INTERNET OF THINGS

FOR ECE STUDENTS UNDER JUT

KH. KAMAL AHMED

Copyright © Kh. Kamal Ahmed
All Rights Reserved.

THIS BOOK IS DEDICATED TO MY SUPPORTIVE WIFE

&

LOVING SON ALI

Contents

CHAPTER ONE

INTRODUCTION TO IoT

IoT and the connected world

In modern era of digital revolution in electronics devices, mainly to connect everyday objects to internet and exchange information, IoT plays a vital role.

IoT network provides an interconnected environment where objects have a digital interference and can communicate with the other objects and people.

An IoT has its own ecosystem where anyone present anywhere and simultaneously can use service/application to control the connected things like connected home: home owner can open smart door locks for an unauthorized person after checking on smart video camera over the internet.

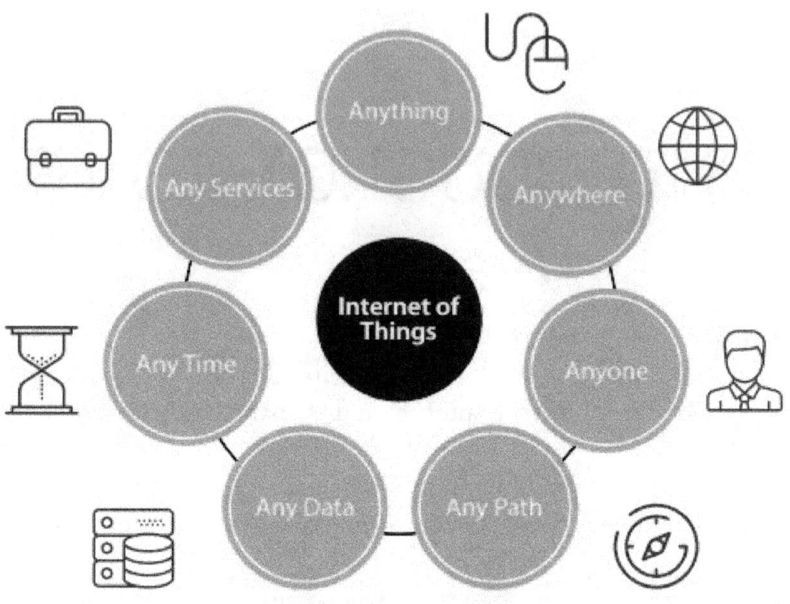

IoT

IoT represents a revolutionary transformation in Information Technology (IT) and digital world that has the potential to touch everyone's life. We can already feel changes to the day-to-day activities such as smart connected homes, smart cities, tagging cattle in agriculture fields, efficient energy management, remotely real-time patients monitoring, integrated supply chain, smart wearable devices, parking sensors and many more.

The growth and adoption of IoT is moving at a very fast rate. Its adoption is driven by multiple forces involving rise in connected devices, evolution of wireless protocols, low-cost micro-processors, huge volumes of data and increase in inclination towards cloud-based application software.

Architecture of IoT

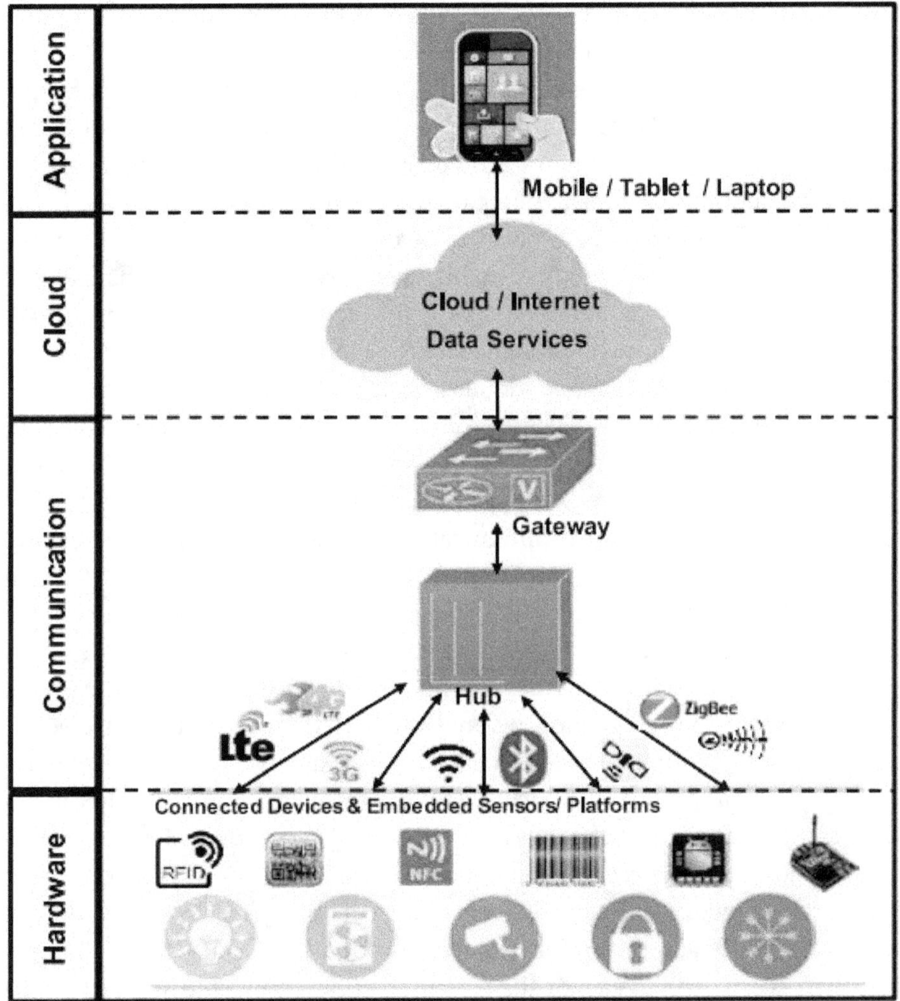

ARCHITECTURE OF IoT

IoT enables are (a) Hardware (smart devices) (b) Communication Layer (c) Cloud (application hosting, rule engine and database etc.) and (d) Application Layer.

Connected physical devices such as embedded devices, sensors, smart meters, actuators, hub, centralized console, gateway and exchange required data to enable connected things.

Data is communicated and transported to network using communication technologies (wi-fi, LTE, 3G, 4G, LAN, WAN etc.)

The IoT architecture mainly focused on:

Device-to-Device: This model uses small data packets of information with low data rate. Home automation or Residential IoT devices like light bulbs, switches and door locks are considered under this category where very small amount of information can be shared.

Device-to-Cloud: This model involves clouding concept where the devices are connected directly to an internet cloud service to exchange data. Through wi-fi, ethernet connections the device will establish connection to the internet and IP network connects to the cloud service.

Device-to-Gateway: This model involves a channel to reach cloud service. An application software on a local gateway device act as an intermediary between the cloud service and the device to provide security and other functionality such as protocol translation. Mainly a smartphone running an application to communicate with the device and relay data to cloud service.

The Most Important Security Problems with IoT Devices:

Incorrect access control:

Services offered by an IoT device should only be accessible by the owner and the people in their immediate environment whom they trust. However, this is often insufficiently enforced by the security system of a device. IoT devices may trust the local network to such level that no further authentication or authorisation is required. Any other device that is connected to the same network is also trusted. This is especially a problem when the device is connected to the Internet: everyone in the world can now potentially access the functionality offered by the device. A common problem is that all devices of the same model are delivered with the same default password (e.g. "admin" or "password123"). The firmware and default settings are usually identical for all devices of the same model. Because the credentials for the device – assuming that, as is often the case, they are not changed by the user - are public knowledge, they can be used to gain access to all devices in that series. IoT devices often have a single account or privilege level, both exposed to the user and internally. This means that when this privilege is obtained, there is no further access control. This single level of protection fails to protect against several vulnerabilities.

Overly large attack surface:

Each connection that can be made to a system provides a new set of opportunities for an attacker to discover and exploit vulnerabilities. The more services a device offers over the Internet, the more services can be attacked. This is known as the attack surface. Reducing the attack surface is one of the first steps in the process of securing a system. A device may have open ports with services running that are not strictly required for operation. An attack against such an unnecessary service could easily be prevented by not exposing the service. Services such as Telnet, SSH or a debug interface may play an important role during development but are rarely necessary in production.

Outdated software:

As vulnerabilities in software are discovered and resolved, it is important to distribute the updated version to protect against the vulnerability. This means that IoT devices must ship with up-to-date software without any known vulnerabilities, and that they must have update functionality to patch any vulnerabilities that become known after the deployment of the device. For example, the malware Linux.Darlloz was first discovered late 2013 and worked by exploiting a bug reported and fixed more than a year earlier.

Lack of encryption:

When a device communicates in plain text, all information being exchanged with a client device or backend service can be obtained by a 'Man-in-the-Middle' (MitM). Anyone who is capable of obtaining a position on the network path between a device and its endpoint can inspect the network traffic and potentially obtain sensitive data such as login credentials. A typical problem in this category is using a plain-text version of a protocol (e.g. HTTP) where an encrypted version is available (HTTPS). A Man-in-the-Middle attack where the attacker secretly accesses, and then relays communications, possibly altering this communication, without either party being aware. Even when data is encrypted, weaknesses may be present if the encryption is not complete or configured incorrectly. For example, a device may fail to verify the authenticity of the other party. Even though the connection is encrypted, it can be intercepted by a Man-in-the-Middle attacker. Sensitive data that is stored on a device (at rest) should also be protected by encryption. Typical weaknesses are lack of encryption by storing API tokens or credentials in plain text on a device. Other problems are the usage of weak cryptographic algorithms or using cryptographic algorithms in unintended ways.

Application vulnerabilities:

Acknowledging that software contains vulnerabilities in the first place is an important step in securing IoT devices. Software bugs may make it possible to trigger functionality in the device that was not intended by the developers. In some cases, this can result in the attacker running their own code on the device, making it possible to extract sensitive information or attack other parties. Like all software bugs, security vulnerabilities are impossible to avoid completely when developing software. However, there are methods to avoid well-known vulnerabilities or reduce the possibility of vulnerabilities. This includes best practices to avoid application vulnerabilities, such as consistently performing input validation.

Lack of trusted execution environment:

Most IoT devices are effectively general-purpose computers that can run specific software. This makes it possible for attackers to install their own software that has functionality that is not part of the normal functioning of the device. For example, an attacker may install software that performs a DDoS attack. By limiting the functionality of the device and the software it can run, the possibilities to abuse the device are limited. For example, the device can be restricted to connect only to the vendor's cloud service. This restriction would make it ineffective in a DDoS attack since it can no longer connect to arbitrary target hosts. To limit the software a device can run, code is typically signed with a cryptographic hash. Since only the vendor has the key to sign the software, the device will only run software distributed by the vendor. This way, an attacker can no longer run arbitrary code on a device. To totally restrict the code run on the device, code signing must also be implemented in the boot process, with the help of hardware. This can be difficult to implement correctly. So called 'jailbreaks' in devices such as the Apple iPhone, Microsoft Xbox and Nintendo Switch are the result of errors in the implementation of trusted execution environments.

Vendor security posture:

When security vulnerabilities are found, the reaction of the vendor greatly determines the impact. The vendor has a role to receive input on potential vulnerabilities, develop a mitigation, and update devices in the field. The vendor security posture is often determined by whether the vendor has a process in place to adequately handle security issues. The consumer mainly perceives the vendor security posture as improved communication with the vendor in relation to security. When a vendor does not provide contact information or instructions how to take action in case of reporting a security issue, it will likely not help to mitigate the issue. Without knowledge of limitations, end users will continue to use the device in the method intended. This may result in a less secure environment. Vendors could make things easier for customers by advising of the frequency of device security updates, and how to securely dispose or resell the device so that sensitive data is not passed on.

User Interaction:

Vendors can encourage secure deployment of their devices by making it easy to configure them securely. By giving proper attention to usability, design, and documentation, users can be nudged into configuring secure settings. There is partial overlap between this category and other categories listed above. For example, the problem of incorrect access control mentioned above includes using unsafe or default passwords. One way to solve this is to make the user interaction with the device such that it is very easy or even mandatory to configure a secure password. For most of the above security categories, it is difficult for a non-technical user to evaluate whether a device meets the requirement. However, user interaction can, by definition, be perceived by the end-user, and so the consumer can evaluate how well a device performs on user interaction. User interaction is an important category to make sure implemented security measures are activated and correctly used. If it is possible to change the default password, but the user does not know or cannot discover the functionality, it is useless.

The top security problems are without a doubt related to access control and exposed services. Furthermore, IoT devices should implement best-practice security measures such as encryption. Vendors can facilitate secure use of their products by providing documentation and interacting with users and security professionals. To make it harder for attackers, devices should be physically secured. Finally, if a device is compromised it should reject programs supplied by the attacker, and notify its user that something is wrong.

Focussing on these problems can certainly improve the state of security of IoT devices. To solve these problems, many Cyber Security agencies recommend vendors to follow a security framework, or propose essential requirements for securing consumer IoT devices.

Opportunities for IoT

A cursory look at Google trends searches for Internet of Things or IoT rightfully shows that the general interest has grown since last one year or so. IoT has started to permeate into our collective consciousness in an awesome way! The world expects IoT to create a hyper-connected network of things. We are well aware of the value which connected networks brings (think Internet), and the fact that technology adoption is itself accelerating at an amazing pace.

A deeper look into what is pushing the growth of IoT

1) Increased availability of affordable smartphone (Smartphones will be crucial even in the IoT era as a personal control hub)
2) Hardware supply chain ecosystem growth due to drop in cost of components like sensors (spurred by smartphones)
3) Focus of semiconductor companies on IoT by providing products for various use cases
4) Increased corporate and government investments in IoT and related opportunities (e.g. Smart cities, Digital India)
5) Hypergrowth in the developers/start-up ecosystem (includes the Investor community)
6) Allied factors like Cloud services (& storage), Big Data & Analytics and growth of API adoptions

One of the key elements in play here is the increasing smartphone penetration, making India second biggest smartphone market in the world. This growth of mobile devices plays a significant role as India is a mobile only country. As the digital divide between HAVEs and HAVE-NOTs diminishes, it also sets the tone for the next wave of technology adoption like IoT, gradually bridging the gap between the online and offline worlds. NASSCOM predicts that India will get minimum 20 percent of the Global IoT revenues of $300 billion.

"IOT is not only going to benefit large enterprise there will be an immense opportunity for start – up developers to showcase their innovations."

For this to happen, there are multiple players from hardware, cloud service, security, telecom, and others working in tandem. Government interest and push from programs such as Digital India, Smart cities and Start-up India Stand-up India are further contributing to the growing number of IoT developers and start-ups across the country.

IoT is not only going to benefit large enterprises, there will be an immense opportunity for start-up developers to showcase their innovations. Gartner had predicted that 50 percent of global IoT solutions will originate in start-ups that are less than three years old. The number of start-ups in India is expected to scale up quickly from 3,100 start-ups in 2014 to a projection of more than 11,500 by 2020, and IoT start-ups are expected to grow fast.

A 2015 study by Progress says that 58 percent of developers expect the IoT to expand beyond smartphones and tablets within two years and most of them see mass adoption of IoT apps occurring within the next five years. Semiconductor companies can directly play a role by helping developers create innovative IoT applications or by providing assistance in using IoT products and services and connecting them to start-ups and businesses across sectors such as agriculture, health-care or retail.

With the increased push for IoT adoption, there are some challenges that need to be overcome as well. Given below are a few:

1. Fragmentation of standards with new ones emerging every day creates a complex situation for an observer. However, as we have seen from the early days of the internet, there will be harmonization of standards and the emergence of a de-facto industry standard over a period of time.

2. Security is another cause for concern in connected devices, especially when it involves sharing of personal information. There is an increased awareness about security and steps taken to prevent attacks; however, threats evolve and are more sophisticated.

3. It is crucial that value is extracted from IoT through cost savings and better service delivery.

Over and above, these three global challenges, there are some India-specific challenges as well.

4. One of the major challenges in India is the Internet connectivity. With a varying availability of connection across the nation, IoT may not be

recognized equally in urban and rural areas which can hinder the growth of the digital nation. This situation should improve as the Government rolls out the plan to connect all 2.5 lakh gram panchayats in the country with a high-speed digital highway using optical fibre.

5. Another deterrent to the adoption of IoT into many sectors could be the lack of skilled workforce for implementation of nationwide IoT systems. As per the Labour Bureau Report of 2014, the skilled workforce in India is only two percent, which is much lower when compared to the developing nations and the number of persons aged 15 years who have the skill or will be trained in a skill is merely 6.8 percent. In order to support this growing ecosystem, the government will need to introduce and support education programs that will help deliver necessary skill-set required.

IoT has become a dynamic driver of innovation and has been accepted by all, however, as per World Economic Forum, manufacturing organizations tend to be early adopters of new innovations. Today, any organization - regardless of size or industry - can harness IoT to deliver new services, elevate customer relationships and unlock new recurring revenue streams with the help of the synergies between domain experts and IoT experts that deal with hardware, software, apps, cloud, security and many others.

We are on the initial leg of the journey to realize the promise of IoT, the new capabilities that businesses and individuals will gain by leveraging connected devices and keep the efforts moving forward at a faster pace to create a massive market opportunity.

CHAPTER TWO

THE WEB OF THINGS

Web of Things is a web standard of the Internet of Things to enable communication between smart things and web-based applications. The major portion of the WoT specification is the Thing Description. Thing is an abstract representation of a physical or virtual entity. A Thing Description includes the metadata and interfaces of a Thing in a standardized way, with the aim to make the Thing able to communicate with other Things in a heterogeneous world. According to the WoT standard, the behavior of a Thing can be expressed by describing the interaction between the consumer and the Thing. This is known as Interaction Affordances, which is a property of objects that can show users what actions they can carry through.

What is the Web of Things?

The concept of the Web of Things was first introduced by researchers around 2007. It has since been adopted and promoted by organizations like Mozilla, Siemens, and the World Wide Web Consortium (W3C). These organizations have established interest groups to define the standards that should govern the Web of Things. This includes the Web Thing Model, which represents a standardized way to provide information on a virtual or physical device, known as a Thing.

Linked data in WoT:

The Internet of Things (IoT) consists of many devices and services producing or consuming data over a network, and, by extension, the internet. There are various protocols and data models used by different vendors of things, or middleware, to expose data and APIs to communicate with and consume data of things. The Web of Things (WoT) addresses IoT's fragmentation by forming a Web-based abstraction layer capable of interconnecting existing IoT platforms, devices, and cloud services and complementing available standards. Specifications of the Web of Things describe data and interaction models exposed to applications, and communication and security requirements for platforms to communicate effectively. At the core of the WoT specifications is the Thing Description, a semantic description of the data and interaction model(s) for a Thing. This helps other Things to perform actions on a Thing, e.g., read or write its properties (the data or state of a Thing). We believe that the WoT can benefit from semantically enhancing a Thing so it contains data values, or state, in the form of self-describing data. This allows powerful semantic processing and reasoning upon its state, and possibly the history of its states. To enable this, we propose a rule-based approach to generate self-describing data from a Thing's state(s).

Enterprise data in WoT:

According to research by Gartner, there will be 6.4 billion connected devices in 2016, up 30% from 2015. Within enterprises, these include generic or cross-industry devices as well as vertical-specific devices that are found only within particular industries.

As the Internet of Things (IoT) has pushed enterprise data from both types of devices into the forefront of critical global business decisions, the stakes of automation have dramatically increased. In order for corporations to leverage the benefits of the IoT's always-on, data-gathering connectivity, they have to ensure that quality, properly governed data are driving the best business strategies possible.

Increasing Data Quality and Incorporating New Data Streams

The data generated from a device on the factory floor being used in the production pipeline may include large amounts of information but it is only valuable if it is accurate. In the connected world, data automation can drive inventory and essentially run the business. The use of "smart" data such as real-time warehouse conditions, inventory fluctuations and asset feedback are often funneled into enterprise resource planning (ERP) and other corporate systems, but whether they are accurate and relevant can have extraordinarily expensive consequences for the enterprise.

Businesses need to ensure that the data driving the business processes is correct and relevant for real-time business decisions. With high data volumes and pipelines accessing data quickly, the process can break down exponentially faster. Due to the speed of automation, businesses simply can't afford to make mistakes.

Quality data is critical for advancing businesses that are highly data-driven, especially with regards to manufacturing, supply chain and the movement of goods. As the IoT becomes more ubiquitous and the streams of data increase, businesses need be prepared to fully integrate the quality data into their business model.

Ensuring Data Governance: Setting and Enforcing Policy

How can a company ensure that the data being collected is accurate at its core? With the rise in the IoT, there are increased security issues around who owns the data, who has access to seeing the data, and the source of the data. Good data governance ensures good data quality, i.e., data that are both correct and relevant to the company's operations.

There is currently momentum towards improving application data management and data governance to be able to set and enforce policy on the data. Enterprise policies should be applied to all data streams working within the system to ensure consistent results. For example, for businesses that rely heavily on data to know when inventory gets low or which products were shipped in the last 12 hours, it is critical to manage and govern data in a way that is compatible with the rest of the business strategy.

With the rise of the IoT, there are great amounts of data coming from a variety of different source systems. The data are subsequently used downstream to drive reports that will eventually help shape decisions affecting the overall business. For example, many enterprises use RFIDs to track the merchandise leaving warehouses and being delivered. Others gather data that can be used for preventive maintenance to the entire system and warns about imminent problems.

For both of these examples, if a problem arises, a data governance system would detect the issue and inform the data owner about the policy breach and they could take action based on pre-determined workflows and scenarios previously set forth in the governance solution.

Another major aspect of data governance is establishing ownership of various data so that they can be deemed reliable. Proper data governance enables businesses to be confident that the company's policies are being executed and that issues with process or reporting that occur downstream from the data collection point can be traced back to the point of origin. Any problem along the pipeline can be pinpointed and notifications can be disseminated so that the business can run properly.

Best practice enterprise governance addresses data quality issues, data errors that can develop from malfunctioning machines and noncompliance that can arise when multiple systems or data sets come together from different connected sources.

If any enterprise data is incorrect, irrelevant or incompatible with the rest of the company's systems, the whole process can break down and result in a high volume of errors and wasted capital. More interconnected devices and technology systems deliver the promise to significantly accelerate supply chain, customer fulfillment, manufacturing, logistics and other areas of business across the globe. Governance that can set and enforce company data policy, coupled with the proper steps for establishing ongoing quality, reliable data, should be the end-goal for those wishing to reap the benefits of IoT into the future.

IoT vs WoT

While the Internet of Things and Web of Things both essentially serve the same purpose of connecting smart devices over the Internet, there are some critical differences between them. These differences are defined by the purpose each one serves and the implementations they involve.

The main difference between IoT and WoT is the layer at which each establishes interconnectivity between devices. In this case, IoT solves just the network layer between devices. That is, each device has a transport medium over which to communicate. To use the example of a highway, IoT represents the road on which cars travel from place to place. It is purely the transportation medium for information to travel from point to point. It is not concerned with how data travels over it or what it intends to do when it reaches its destination. Because of this, the IoT itself cannot help guide information to its destination or coordinate between different data sources. This is where IoT's limitations begin to become apparent.

In contrast to IoT's network layer solutions, WoT can be thought of as the application layer. It sits on top of the IoT conceptually and functionally. WoT is not an alternative or competitor to IoT; instead, it tries to enhance IoT. It does this by defining standard definitions and models for representing devices on the Internet. In the highway analogy, WoT represents the street signs, traffic lights, and engineered routes that establish the rules of the road. It exists to establish well-defined paths for data to travel between points and ensure that it is compatible with its source and destination.

WoT enables devices to connect over the web using mainstream technologies and standards from a technical perspective—for example, HTML 5.0 and JavaScript. The WoT paradigms promote RESTful API designs, a common Internet standard for application development.

In summary, WoT evolves IoT from a pure concept to a fully-developed architectural approach for smart device interaction. It serves to define standards for IoT-enabled devices to communicate better.

WoT Architecture

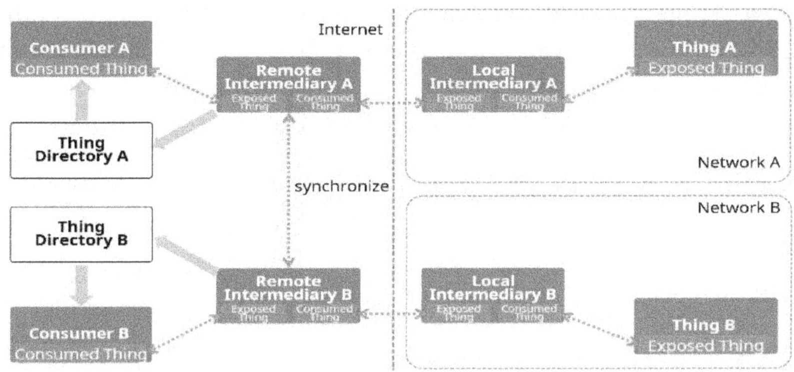

WoT ARCHITECTURE

The World Wide Web is composed of many different evolving architectural standards. The Web of Things architecture has been contributed to by many organizations, but it is spearheaded by the World Wide Web Consortium (W3C), an established group to establish web standards. The W3C's standardization of WoT is based on several building blocks. These are the Thing Description, Binding Templates, Scripting API, and Security and Privacy Guidelines.

The WoT Thing Description is the basis upon which IoT devices ("Things") can fit into WoT. The Thing Description defines the metadata and interfaces that a Thing should provide. This definition produces a format for metadata that is guaranteed to be machine-readable in compliance with the standard.

Protocol Bindings refer to the protocols over which IoT devices communicate. The W3C attempts to establish, therefore, the standard interfaces to interact with these protocols with Binding Templates. These Binding Templates allow unique Thing Descriptions to be modeled after and interact with different established protocols for communication.

The WoT Scripting API provides a common programming language for implementing Thing connectivity over IoT. This API is in the form of a

JSON API. A device doesn't need to use the Scripting API to be part of the WoT, but it is convenient to simplify application portability across platforms.

Finally, the Security and Privacy Guidelines are perhaps the most important aspect of WoT. Much like the Internet itself does not define any specific safety guidelines for applications, neither does the Internet of Things. In a technical world where cyber-attacks and compromised personal electronic security are becoming a threat, ensuring that data is safe is more important than ever. This becomes especially true when physical devices are connected to the Internet. These devices can be directly connected to homes, offices, or even medical applications. This is why W3C has laid out the Security and Privacy Guidelines for developers to implement standard safety practices in Internet-connected devices.

While the WoT architecture is very detailed, it is founded on these basic concepts. These four components comprise the basic layout of WoT.

WoT Use Cases and Applications

With the prevalent adoption of IoT already in use, one may wonder if there are any practical reasons for this newer application layer in the real world. There are, in fact, many use cases for WoT standards in commercial, residential, and industrial capacities.

Many people will interact with WoT through smart home technologies. A smart home is inherently dependent on many different devices communicating, either directly or through the cloud. Thermostats, doors, security cameras, and even smoke detectors need to be reachable by homeowners. WoT ensures that these devices all speak the "same language" when working together.

In a commercial application, many of the exact needs still apply. WoT-enabled production facilities, smart factories can take advantage of machinery connected to the Internet. This allows automated production capabilities and remote monitoring of that production. That monitoring can also ensure the safety of factory conditions, much like the security cameras and smoke detectors that help keep families safe at home.

The possibilities of a standardized Internet of connected Things are endless. Agriculture, logistics, construction, transportation, and municipalities can all benefit from the advancements of smart device technology. These industries often overlap, so the interconnectivity of their devices with other businesses is essential to the smooth operation of the supply chain. WoT ensures that devices can communicate not just within one use case but also across use cases seamlessly.

WoT Challenges

While WoT seeks to solve many IoT problems, it does come with its challenges. No technology is perfect, and there are, of course, tradeoffs to certain gains. WoT is no exception to this.

The main concern with WoT is security and privacy. As mentioned above, putting anything onto the Internet risks losing due to web application vulnerabilities. That risk is even more serious when there is a direct physical link to the real world. The W3C's Security and Privacy Guidelines outline best practices for mitigating these risks. However, those guidelines are public, which poses the possibility that hackers could find loopholes in them. Also, when many devices follow the same standard, any weakness in that standard exposes every device to the same vulnerability.

Besides security, WoT devices could suffer from energy inefficiency. A home or business that is fully connected to WoT will require many devices to be using electricity 24/7. This round-the-clock operation is essential so that the device can activate at any time it is needed. Of course, this can be mitigated by identifying peak times when devices need to be active. But for certain use cases, such as security and safety systems.

That need for constant availability is also a potential vector for failure. Denial-of-service (DoS) attacks can render devices inoperable, even if they are powered on all the time. In a DoS attack, hackers continuously send signals to a device to occupy its resources so that legitimate requests cannot be processed. The attack can lock valid users out of their own devices or even crash the devices for as long as the attackers have the resources to continue sending requests.

The good news about WoT is that, as an open standard, it is always being innovated by the most active technical contributors who specialize in these areas. Because of that, security concerns and drawbacks can be solved over time as the standards improve. Even today, many of these risks are only minor, thanks to the hard work that has already been put in to set up the security guidelines of WoT.

The Future of WoT

The IoT has been a revolutionary shift in the perception of the types of devices that connect to the Internet. It is no longer assumed that only computers can communicate over the web. Now, all types of devices, appliances, and tools can be programmed with the ability to improve their usability thanks to the Internet. This pervasive paradigm shift has evolved even further with the development of the Web of Things.

As the growing capabilities of smart devices led to growing adoption, the need for standardized communication between devices grew as well. This growth shows no signs of slowing, as more and more devices are getting online every day. That's where WoT has stepped in to help guide the changing landscape of smart devices to converge on common protocols for interconnectivity. This standardization will help WoT grow one of the more common trends in web technology.

As the WoT architecture gains adoption among device developers, the capabilities of these devices will increase. Devices will no longer be locked into their vendors, driving competition and innovation between producers. This alone will allow the trends of smart homes, businesses, factories, and cities to continue at an efficient and affordable rate.

CHAPTER THREE

Lessons from the Internet

The Internet of Things (IoT) is a name for the aggregate collection of network-enabled devices, excluding traditional computers like laptops and servers. Types of network connections can include Wi-Fi connections, Bluetooth connections, and near-field communication (NFC). The IoT includes devices such as "smart" appliances, like refrigerators and thermostats; home security systems; computer peripherals, like webcams and printers; wearable technology, such as Apple Watches and Fitbits; routers; and smart speaker devices, like Amazon Echo and Google Home.

Connectivity and networks for the Internet of Things data deluge

Connectivity and computing approaches to leverage the Internet of Things (IoT) from a data and communication perspective.

With the rise of the IoT, there is obviously an avalanche of data being added to the networks and data processing, storage and analysis platforms of this digital world.

Knowing that we are really just at the beginning of the Internet of Things evolution, except perhaps for some industries such as utilities, that is good news for many ICT companies and infrastructure providers. In the field of consumer applications, the IoT today really still is close to nowhere. So, imagine where we're going in an already very data-intensive environment which really is just beginning to see the true impact of the Internet of Things data.

Cloud and network/communication technologies drive evolutions in the Internet of Things

A broad range of companies and service providers is benefiting from yet another data explosion, caused by the Internet of Things. Among them are those that provide the infrastructure and connectivity which is required to transport, store, protect and leverage all this Internet of Things data. Note: not all IoT applications are as data-intensive than those you might find in industrial environments. Internet of Things applications in areas such as smart parking or smart farming have small data needs.

Still, connectivity and networks have to adapt to an IoT world. It's not a coincidence that a company such as Cisco, for instance, is claiming a leading position in the IoT space as, even if it's evolving, its core business is still very much about networks. While numerous new forms of network and connectivity technologies and of course the cloud have enabled, or better accelerated, the rise of the Internet of Things (and vice versa, as the cloud and IoT are strongly linked), IoT also impacts network and infrastructure technology evolutions.

Along with demands for increased capacity and intelligence within networks, as a consequence of digital transformation, there is also a new IT infrastructure paradigm whereby capacity, computing, connectivity and cloud technologies are moving closer to the devices themselves, closer to the edge of the network. Edge computing is the name and it's becoming important. Here as well, Cisco is a key driver with its fog computing.

Evolving network technologies to optimize bandwidth

There isn't one single form of network and data technology that solves all data and analytics challenges and possibilities brought upon us by various usage scenarios in the Internet of Things.

There also isn't a single type of connectivity solution that connects people, things and networks in shorter ranges. As you know, IoT is an umbrella term for many possible applications in many possible industries where several technologies can be more relevant than others and de facto it's always a mix in IoT.

The impact of the nascent deluge of data, mainly unstructured data, coming from the Internet of Things, is a challenge for networks across the globe. In a world where the need for bandwidth already keeps accelerating for a myriad of reasons, ranging from mobile data and video to 'bandwidth-intensive' applications such as videoconferencing and ever bigger files, the challenge is on, for the Internet and for corporate networks.

It's one of the reasons why in the context of Wide Area Networks (WAN) you see a gradual shift towards hybrid networking with added intelligence to optimally use and scale available capacity and a shift towards network function virtualization (NFV) and software-defined networking (SDN) to make networks more available, faster and smarter (read: far more based on software). Connecting millions and soon billions of devices does lead to new WAN technologies indeed.

The connectivity and network technologies for Internet of Things data

Next to these evolutions in network technologies, which are about more than just the Internet of Things but about ongoing digitization in general, there are also the numerous connectivity technologies which are more related with the Internet of Things itself.

From Bluetooth and NFC to WiFi and ZigBee

Examples include short range wireless connectivity solutions such as RFID, NFC, Bluetooth, Wi-Fi and the specific approaches of a bunch of probably less familiar sounding things such as ZigBee, Z-Wave (for home automation) or UWB (Ultra Wide-Band).

Moreover, as mentioned, in some circumstances you need mobile networks or even satellite connections (an example at the bottom of this page) – and here again, there are additional flavors and standards.

Cellular IoT

Cellular networks play a big role too.

	15 billion	28 billion	CAGR 2015–2021
Cellular IoT	0.4	1.5	27%
Non-cellular IoT	4.2	14.2	22%
PC/laptop/tablet	1.7	1.8	1%
Mobile phones	7.1	8.6	3%
Fixed phones	1.3	1.4	0%
	2015	2021	

CELLULAR IoT

There will be approximately 28 billion connected devices in 2021 (according to Ericsson) and cellular IoT will grow from 0.4 billion devices connected via cellular networks in 2015 to 1.5 billion in 2021, representing a CAGR of 27 percent as you can see in the graphic.

In the context of cellular IoT we need to mention 5G in IoT*(and depending on use case 2, 3 and 4G)*, LTE-M or LTE-MTC, NB LTE-M and NB-IoT (the latter two also classified under LPWAN technologies, see below). According to many NB-IoT is a potential killer of the low power wide area (LPWA) technologies, which operate in the unlicensed spectrum and which we cover below. Vodafone is pushing hard to get NB-IoT out everywhere *(with Huawei)*.

However, with the IoT it's not different than in other technologies: rarely there is a one-size-fits all. An example: Cisco has an offering which combines LPWAN (LoRa, see below), WiFi and cellular IoT into its own LoRaWAN offering.

LPWA(N) and beyond

Time to talk about these LPWA/LPWAN technologies. On top of cellular IoT, there are several other wireless network technologies, designed for the Internet of things.

As you might know many components of a longer-range Internet of Things ecosystem such as sensors require little power and sometimes use data which are sent for a long period but with longer intervals and at a relatively low bit rate. LPWAN, which is wireless, can offer the connectivity which such devices need for a longer period of time as it is also low-power. There are various LPWAN platforms/technologies, including for example machine-to-machine *(M2M)* technology Weightless, Ingenu *(with its RMPA technology for IoT and M2M)*, France-based Sigfox and LoRA/LoRaWan. As said, these wireless IoT connectivity solutions operate in the unlicensed spectrum, whereas cellular IoT does not.

MANAGEMENT AND SECURITY CHALLENGES:

The Internet of Things (IoT) brings connectivity to about every object found in the physical space. It extends connectivity to everyday objects. From connected fridges, cars and cities, the IoT creates opportunities in numerous domains. However, this increase in connectivity creates many prominent challenges. This paper provides a survey of some of the major issues challenging the widespread adoption of the IoT. Particularly, it focuses on the interoperability, management, security and privacy issues in the IoT. It is concluded that there is a need to develop a multifaceted technology approach to IoT security, management, and privacy.

The Internet of Things (IoT) goes beyond the typical computer-based-Internet model to a distributed heterogeneous model of connected things.

The state-of-the-art application in the IoT provides IoT services based on utilizing and combining data received from various things. It is a complex system that has the capabilities of sensing information about the environment, capabilities of collecting physiological measurements, and machine operational data, abilities of identifying users, animals, other things, and events in an environment; and the capabilities of processing and communicating these data with other things. Also, it has the capabilities of converting the data into automated instructions that feedback through the communication networks to other things with actuating capabilities. These things will in turn actuate other things, eliminating many human interference roles. Clearly, with such a diverse, complex and heterogeneous model of the IoT, numerous challenges arise. To realize the unique and futuristic characteristics of the IoT, management and security of things, should be well thought-out as one of the fundamental enablers of this technology. There is a need to manage the unprecedented number of things connected to the Internet that generate a large amount of traffics, particularly things with low resources. With billions of things equipped with sensors and actuators entering the digital word using a vast array of technologies, incorporated into devices like lights, electric appliances, home automation systems and a vast number of other integrated machinery devices, transport vehicles, and equipment; management of things become a necessity and cumbersome task.

Network-based Integration

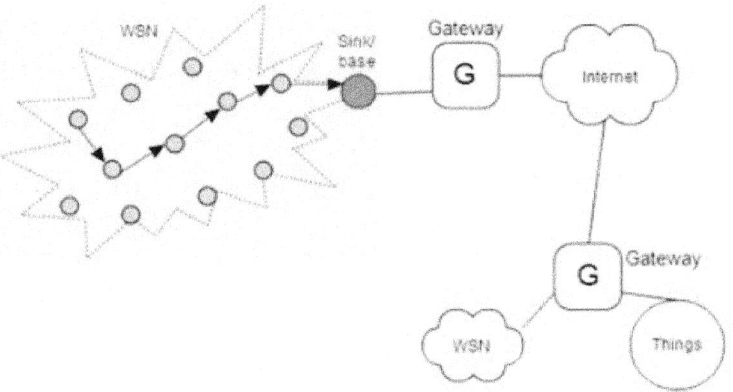

NETWORK BASED INTEGRATION

In the Network-based Integration topology, the sensors join the Internet through their network gateway as shown in above Figure. In the case of a multi-hop mesh wireless topology, the sensors rely on a base node, also known as a sink, which even possesses gateway's capabilities or have a connection with a gateway. The sensors, in this case, are not directly accessible on the Internet. Communications between a sensor of a particular Wireless Sensor Network (WSN) and that of another WSN or/ and with other things on the IoT are not going to be direct but via the WSN's base node.

Independent Integration

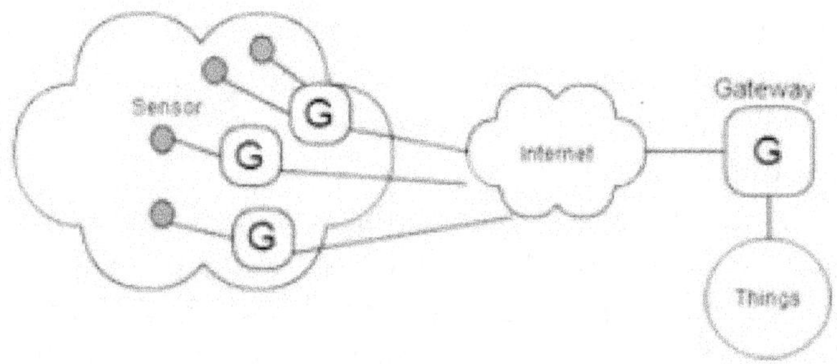

Independent Integration

In the Independent Integration topology, the sensors can connect directly to the Internet independently from their base point. As a result, the interaction between an independent sensor and other things in the IoT can be established without the need to pass by the intermediate node (i.e., the sink node in the WSN). The topology of such a communication network is given in above Figure. However, giving an IP address to every sensor, for the purpose of connecting to the Internet, may not be the right approach. This is because wireless sensors communications are generally characterized by their low-cost and low-power features with packets exchanged periodically and in small sizes. Therefore, it is quite challenging to provide every IoT device with an IP address to connect to the Internet. This is due to the communication and processing overheads associated with the use of the TCP protocol that challenges the capabilities of small and low-cost sensors.

Hybrid Integration

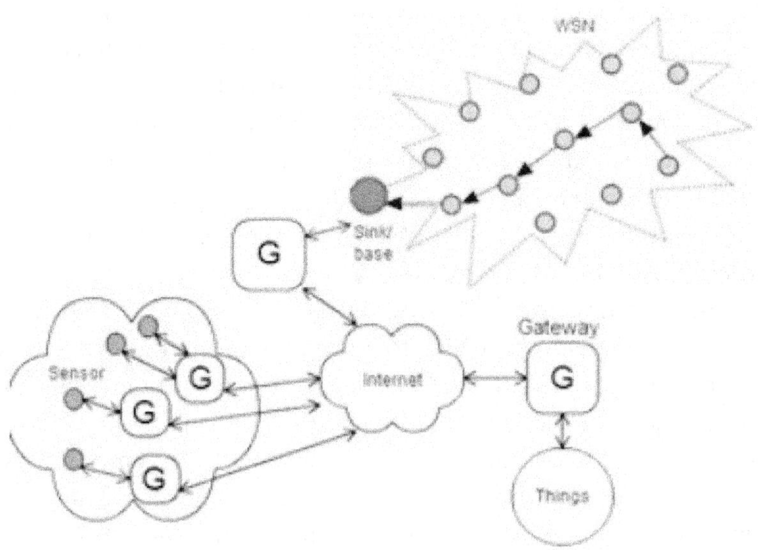

Hybrid Integration

The above Figure shows the "hybrid integration" topology. In this topology, the IoT integrates WSNs using a mixture of the previously introduced topologies.

Other Interoperability Challenges

A typical IoT system has been repetitively described in this book as a system collecting and making use of shared data among things. However, for a basic communication to occur, a user or device needs a way to search for things and access the data they produce. This requires an agreement on many fundamental communication issues such as those relating to how things are represented, searched and accessed on the Internet. Additionally, there are associated issues which need to be considered as well. These issues relate to security (authorization, authentication, trust, integrity, validation, etc.), and privacy including privacy of the users and devices. Therefore, to achieve interoperability in the IoT, several other associated challenges need to be considered as well, including the followings:

Thing Interaction: As discussed in the previous section, there is more than one option to how things will interact with other things or the users. There exist situations where interactions with individual things are needed.

On the other hand, there exist situations where the ability to query and control large groups of things at the same time is also required.

Virtual Representation of Things: How things are represented, and described remains an issue unsolved or precisely unstandardized. For instance, do we need to establish a shared schema or ontology for things for greater interoperability? Which attributes should be used to describe things and how flexible and unified this descriptor system should be? Can we find appropriate ways to involve users in connecting things and resolving ambiguities based on their current operation or context?

Searching, Finding and Accessing Things: How do we search for things on the Internet? Should we be able to search for things by their unique ID, IP, location, name or/and in combination with other properties? How can we discover, search, locate or track mobile things that may move from one location or network to another? How should things be organized, deployed, managed and secured? Syntactic Interoperability between Things: Recall that syntactic interoperability deals with the packaging and transmission mechanisms for data over a network. Thus, when all the above challenges are addressed, there will still be a need to ensure that data flow is interoperable between the various networks and among a mixture of devices. Translation functionalities in networks or in some devices, gateways or in the form of middleware sitting on the edge of a network are most likely needed.

MANAGEMENT CHALLENGES

Traditionally, network management solutions are needed to manage network equipment, devices, and services. However, with the IoT, there is a need to manage not only the traditional networked devices and their services, but also an entirely new range of things. The enormous number of things and their diversity create many management requirements. Thus, traditional management functionalities such as remote control, monitoring and maintenance are considered of paramount significance for the operation of things in the IoT. However, these management capabilities need to evolve to cater for the unique characteristics of the IoT. This is because the IoT is of a diverse nature supporting heterogeneous communications and seamless machine to machine interactions. This is in addition to the specific management capabilities required for managing things in the IoT. For example, self-configuration and network reconfiguration are essential management requirements in the IoT. On the other hand, traditionally, network management solutions aimed at providing management information within a minimal response time. However, in some IoT scenarios which might involve lightweight devices, management solutions should provide comprehensive management information with minimal energy use. Nevertheless, the characteristics of data generated in the IoT are distinct from other data in use today.

For instance, IoT data have been described as having five distinct characteristics: Heterogeneity, Inaccuracy of sensed data, Scalability and Semantics. We add minimal or constrained as another important feature governing data in the IoT as, generally, things in the IoT have limited computation, communication, and power resources at their disposal. Additionally, in the context of IoT, data management systems must summarize data online from multiple heterogeneous sources while providing storage, logging, and auditing facilities for offline analysis. Therefore, management functionalities are needed to allow managers to perform many maintenance tasks remotely over the Internet and possibly across many heterogeneous interconnected networks. Such management capabilities help in reducing errors and accelerating response time. The ability to turn things on and off, disconnecting things from specific networks, and monitoring the statuses of things are amongst the important tasks that a management system should support.

On the other hand, having a management system deployed in an IoT network helps in eliminating travel's and staff training's costs. Also, it helps in accelerating the response to failure events. For example, a management system that supports the remote monitoring, via the Internet, of sensors and other smart devices deployed in remote locations or a busy city is highly beneficial and essential in emergency applications. Such a system allows managers to remotely control, diagnose errors, and troubleshoot IoT devices in real time, reducing costs and accelerating many maintenance tasks. Furthermore, the magnitude of network connections and data associated with the IoT poses additional challenges in terms of data and service management. These challenges relate to data collection and aggregation, provisioning of services and control as well as monitoring the performance of things. Thus, performance becomes significant in IoT applications that deploy things in remote locations where accessibility is an issue. Performance is also considered important in emergency applications where failure can be catastrophic. Thus, management solutions should provide the capabilities needed to monitor the performance of things and the IoT network as well. Performance statistics relating to response time, availability, up and down time, and others are also highly advantageous. Other performance requirements relate to things' hardware. This is because, providing insights into the health of things, and their networks are an important performance activity. For instance, monitoring and reporting the change in things' state (e.g., the status of an actuator whether it is running or no), the ambience's temperature, hardware's temperature, battery levels, among others, are necessary for the overall management of things in the IoT.

The below mentioned points describes the major management issues challenging the IoT.

Configuration Management
- How things are setup and by whom?
- Network connectivity
- Self-configuration capability.
- Asynchronous Transaction Support.
- Network reconfiguration.

Things' control

Management issues including turning things on and off, disconnecting things from specific networks and connecting to other. To effectively control a thing, a prior knowledge of the thing's status is required. Therefore, "Things' control" complements "monitoring of things."

Monitoring

It is essential for the operation and control of things to know the status of things e.g., running, listening, down, sleep mode, etc. Therefore, once things are deployed and in use, there should be a way to monitor their statuses.

These are in addition to:
- Network status monitoring
- Network topology discovery.
- Notification.
- Logging.

Things' maintenance:

Detecting the failure of a thing is important, specifically in an IoT network which might involve a larger number of things. A tool or software is required for detecting and addressing things' failure. Other issues relate to the general maintenance tasks of things e.g., software update, patch update, protocols version detections, etc.

Things' performance

Monitoring the performance of things is needed so sign of stress can be detected before the occurrence of any failure. This is significant for things that might be deployed in remote locations, and essential in emergency applications, where availability and other QoS parameters are of high importance.

Things' security and privacy

There are basic security challenges such as authorization, authentication and access control that need to be addressed. Security bootstrapping mechanisms are also required. Other security issues are associated with things-to-things communications. For instance, if things are to be accessed by applications or software independently from the human users, then there are security measures that need to be enforced to ensure that things are not leaking information and disclosing private information to unauthorized things or used miscellaneously. Things have their users and owners. Thus, privacy is vital as well.

Energy Management

• Management of energy resources.

• Statistics on energy levels, e.g., estimated lifespan.

SECURITY CHALLENGES

The growth in the number of connected devices to the communication networks in the IoT translates into increased security risks and poses new challenges to security. A device which connects to the Internet, whether it is a constraint or smart device, inherits the security risks of today's computer devices. Almost all security challenges are found in the IoT. Hence, some fundamental security requirements in the IoT such as authorization, authentication, confidentiality, trust, and data security need to be considered. Therefore, things should be securely connected to their designated network(s), firmly controlled and accessed by authorized entities. Data generated by things need to be collected, analyzed, stored, dispatched and always presented in a secure manner. Nevertheless, there are security risks associated with things-to-things communications as well. This is in addition to the risks relating to things-to-person communications. For instance, if things are to be accessed by things independently from the human users, then there are security measures that need to be enforced. These security measures are necessary to ensure that things are accessed only by authorized entities in a secure manner. Also, they need to ensure that things are not leaking information or disclosing private information to unauthorized things and users, or used miscellaneously.

The Inherited Security Challenges in the IoT

The IoT can be regarded as the Internet 2.0 or the future Internet. Thus, the IoT is not another form of communications or networks running in parallel with what we now today as the Internet; but indeed, an expansion of it. Therefore, the IoT inherits today's Internet security issues and poses some new ones as well. These security issues are discussed in the followings sub-sections.

End-to-End Security

Cisco defines end-to-end security as an absolute requirement for secure communications. It is the process of protecting the communications and data exchanged between both ends of the communication without being read, eavesdropped, intercepted, modified, or tampered. In the IoT, end-to-end security remains an open challenge for many IoT devices and applications. The nature of the IoT with its heterogeneous architecture and devices involve the sharing of information and collaboration between things across many networks. This poses serious challenges to the end-to-end security. When devices have different characteristics and operate using a variety of communication technologies (802.11 vs. 802.15.4), establishing secure sessions and secure communications, become a very complex task to achieve.

Additionally, not all devices in the IoT are equal. Currently, computers, smartphones, and other computerized devices connect to the Internet via HTTP, SMTP and the like for most of their activities. As such Transport Layer Security (TLS) and IP security (IPsec) protocols are usually used to negotiate dynamically the session keys, and to provide the required security functions. However, some of the devices in the IoT do not possess the ability to run TLS and IPsec protocols due to their limited computation and power capabilities. Additionally, some embedded devices in the IoT have limited connectivity as such they may not necessarily use HTTP or even IP for the communications (e.g., a sensor in a WSN).

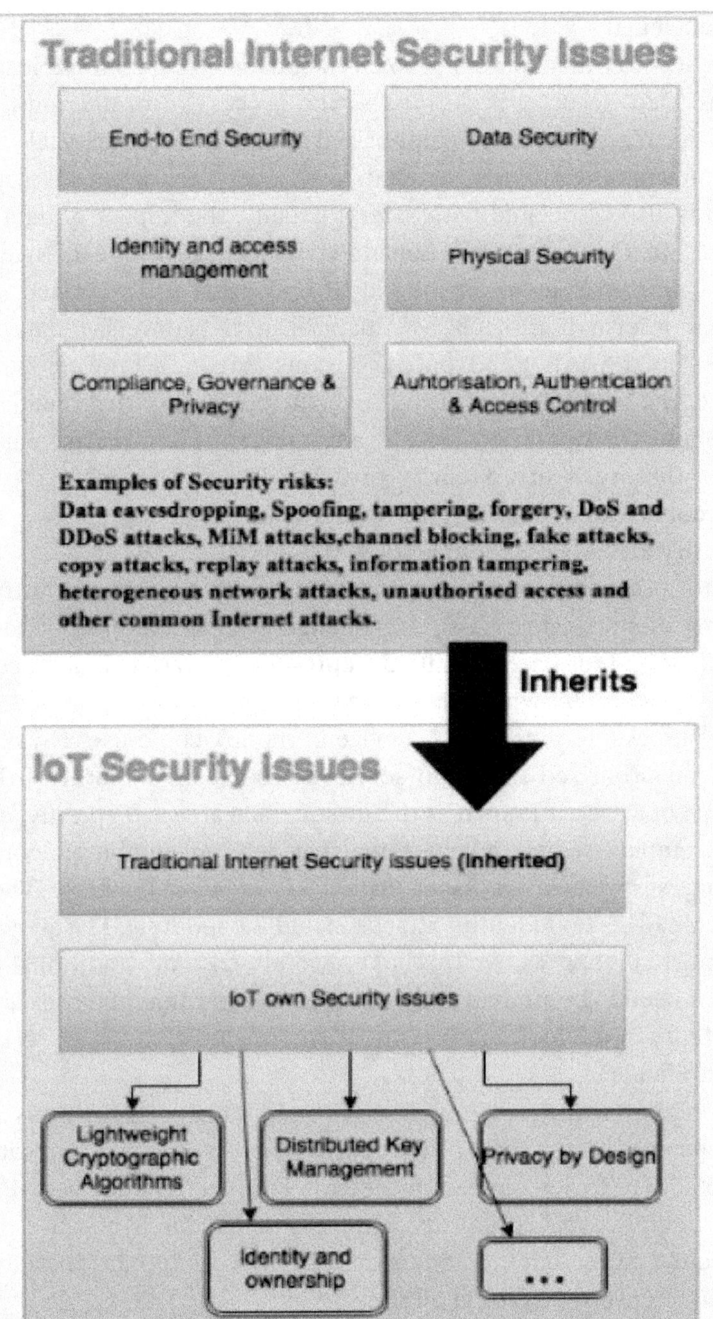

IoT SECURITY

Data Security

Data security involves the protection of data during communications and storages. Data security is defined as the process of protecting data from destructive forces or from unauthorized access. Data security, also referred to as information security, is vital to the IoT security. Data security in the IoT is also associated with safety. Usually, the impact of data security breaches on the human life remained within the scope of hacking the personal information of an individual or getting unauthorized access to sensitive information such as financial data. However, data security breaches in the IoT could pose a serious threat to humans' safety. For instance, the accidental intrusion or malicious access that could interfere or interrupt the operations of a driverless car or a heart pacemaker will threaten the user's life. Security breaches in an IoT forest fire detection system could lead to catastrophic results as well.

Identity and Access Management

Identity theft, forgery, and masquerading among other security attacks are some of the security issues challenging the protection of identity in the IoT. How things are identified, represented, searched, and accessed in the IoT is still unknown. This is indeed making things vulnerable to many identity attacks. For instance, a device in the IoT could uses a fake identity to gain unauthorized access to services provided by another IoT device. This type of attack is known as the masquerade attack. Typically, computer devices employ secure mechanisms that rely on complex algorithms in detecting suspicious access to data and detect imposters. The IoT is vulnerable to several identity attacks including Spoofing, Masquerade, MiM and Smurf attacks as well. Thus, several existent traditional security solutions need to be studied and examined to determine their feasibility and applicability in the IoT.

Compliance

Complying with government laws and industry regulations plays an important role in preserving the security of IoT systems. Things in the IoT need to adhere to several data protection laws and privacy acts. Privacy in the IoT requires special considerations as well. This is because the IoT is built around autonomous communications between things. Therefore, there is a need to ensure privacy at all time.

Initially, privacy requirements can be summarized to three key concepts:

1. User consent: the user needs to be able to provide an informed consent on the usage of their data

2. Freedom of choice: the user should have the freedom of opting in and out from being involved or being part of a communication

3. Anonymity: the user has the right to remain anonymous when obtaining services that do not require identity verification or the like.

Access Control

Access control is the process of granting, limiting or restricting access to a resource. It regulates who or what can view or use resources. Role based access control (RBAC) is an example of a widely used access control model. Access control in the IoT is discussed in more details in a subsequent section. These security issues are derived from the dynamic IoT network structure, the different type of communications involved, and the low-cost characteristic of the IoT devices among other factors which are exclusively associated with the IoT. Significantly, these security issues cannot be solved with traditional Internet security solutions. This is due to the fact that IoT communications' architectures differ from those of the traditional Internet. As the IoT evolves and becomes more complex, the security issues increase in complexity as well. This increase in complexity can be attributed to two fundamental IoT factors: low-cost and heterogeneity.

With regard to low-cost, some IoT devices should be available at relatively low prices. The low-cost of things is a significant factor that drives the support for large-scale deployment of things in the IoT. However, this low-cost requirement dictates that things are mostly resource constrained. This translates into devices with lower computational capabilities, limited amount of memory and power supply. This is, in fact, constitute an obstacle for the application of many traditional cryptographic-based solutions. Given that traditional public-key infrastructures cannot accommodate the IoT.

As of heterogeneity, the diversity of devices and communications in the IoT produce many new security challenges as well. For instance, the integration of WSNs into the Internet, as part of the IoT, creates new security problems. These security problems are derived from the process of connecting a sensor node with an Internet device.

Physical and DoS Security Risks

Traditionally, network equipment requires the protection against physical attacks and against unauthorized accesses e.g., the storage of routers in secure cabinets. In the IoT, many IoT devices require similar protection measures against physical or unauthorized attacks. Hence, strengthening the physical security of things is essential in many IoT applications. The IoT is vulnerable to the Denial of Service (DoS) attack as well. Typically, a DoS attack floods a given server with false requests for services. Thus, it prevents legitimate requesters from accessing the server's services. It attempts to exhaust the computational resources of the server. The IoT vulnerability to the DoS attack is not only limited to things which connect to the Internet directly, but also extend to WSNs. Nodes in a WSN connect to the Internet eventually, despite the topology used in the network. Therefore, WSNs cannot escape DoS attacks. Additionally, the heterogeneous nature and complexity of communications envisioned in the IoT, makes the IoT vulnerable to the distributed denial of service (DDoS) attack. A DDoS is a DoS attack made by multiple agents in the network and from various locations. Therefore, disruptive attacks such as the DoS and DDoS attacks are a serious potential risk to the IoT. Many IoT devices have limited processing capabilities and memory constraints. Therefore, DDoS attacks can easily exhaust their resources. Also, in things- to-things communications, DoS attacks can prove to be difficult to notice before the disruption of the service which could generally be attributed to battery exhaustion.

IoT Security Requirements:

Authorization:

For smart IoT devices, this requirement can be satisfied using traditional authorization techniques. For constrained devices and in low-power wireless networks, such as ZigBee IP, unauthorized access to the IoT devices should be blocked at the coordinator. That's unauthorized requests should not even be routed to the IoT devices as this may exhaust their energy.

Authentication

Authentication simply means verifying that "you are who you are claiming to be". This is usually done using a username and password-based authentication system. However, this system is not secure enough. Passwords usually require frequent changing and it cannot be used with unattended devices. Also, the Secure Sockets Layer protocol (SSL) is used for authentication. (Mainly, a web browser authenticates web sites using SSL). Authentication also include the process of authenticating both the sender and receiver where they are able to verify the origin of the exchanged messages. This is a complicated security requirement in the IoT. This is because things might not necessarily have IP addresses.

Integrity and Freshness

Message integrity is about ensuring a message hasn't been altered. This is extremely important in the IoT as many applications rely on information supplied by things to change the statuses of other things. Freshness is also vital for ensuring that no older messages are replayed.

Confidentiality

Protecting personal and sensitive data from being accessed by unauthorized entities in lightweight devices in the IoT is a challenging task.

In the early days of the Internet which was basically centered on computers, a network of networks was the term used to define the Internet. In the IoT, it seems everything is going to be connected, pants, shoes, shirts, fridges, glasses, washing machines, plants, dogs, cars, airplanes, cities, you name it. Yet, the term network of networks can still be used to define the IoT. However, what's new is that connected networks are no longer limited to IP connected devices/networks in the fashion that we know today. Instead, there are islands of networks connecting using various network technologies. Today, the majority of IoT devices are connected to a mobile phone application. To get anything done, the user has to administer an array of applications in addition to jumping from an application to another in order to control what should be a smart device. We are at risk of creating remote islands of IoT technologies instead of achieving a true vision of IoT. The IoT has the potential of shaping the way we consume energy, improve resources efficiency such as food and water, and support assisted living, access to healthcare, and so much more by connecting different applications together. Therefore, for the realization of a true vision of the IoT, major challenges such as achieving interoperability between the various IoT enabling technologies and devices were identified in this research. Additionally, the main challenge is not only in simply building an IoT system that connects various IoT devices together, but in maintaining scalable, private, secure and trustworthy operations on the IoT. Consequently, it is concluded that there is a need to accommodate the differences in technologies across the various areas of the IoT. For the future advancement of the IoT, it is therefore imperative to develop a multifaceted technology approach to IoT security, interoperability, management and privacy. The internetworking mechanisms of things, WSNs and traditional computer devices in the IoT are vital with respect to standardizing the communications on the Internet. It is also crucial to have lightweight, scalable and adaptive security solutions in place to secure the users' information and preserve their privacy in the IoT.

CHAPTER FOUR

TECHNOLOGIES: WIRELESS PROTOCOLS, CONNECTIVITY OPTIONS

Types of Wireless Communication Protocols in IOT and connectivity:

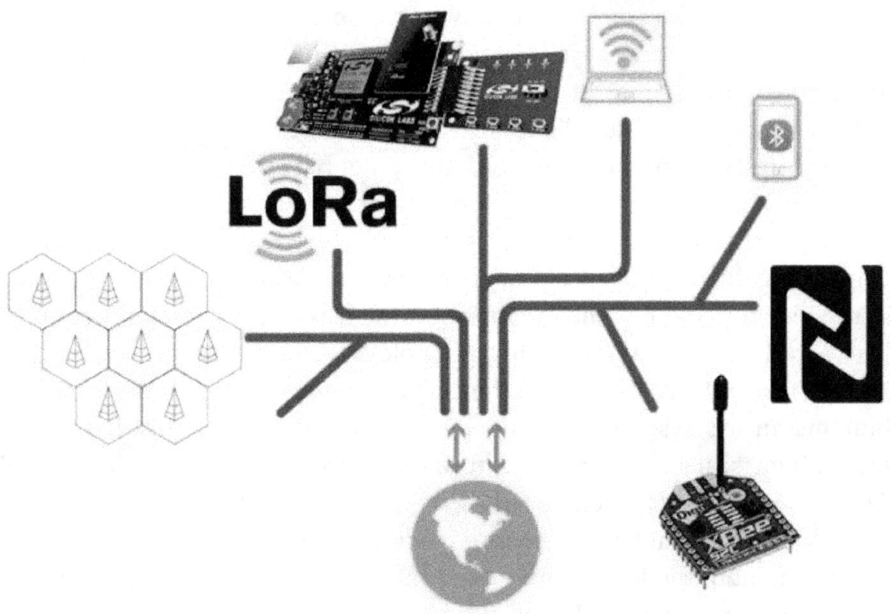

COMMUNICATION PROTOCOL

IoT (Internet of Things) has power to make the complete system automatic. There are various IOT communication protocols which are used in communication between devices in the IoT network. The wireless communication protocol is a standard set of rules with reference to which various electronic devices communicate with each other wirelessly. Since there are many wireless communication protocols available to use for your product, it becomes difficult for the product designers to choose the correct one but once the scope of IoT application is decided it would become easier to select the right protocol. Here some protocols used in IOT with their features and applications are described.

Wi-Fi

WiFi

Wi-Fi (Wireless Fidelity) is the most popular IOT communication protocols for wireless local area network (WLAN) that utilizes the IEEE 802.11 standard through 2.4 GHz UHF and 5 GHz ISM frequencies. Wi-Fi provides Internet access to devices that are within the range of about 20 - 40 meters from the source. It has a data rate up to 600 Mbps maximum, depending on channel frequency used and the number of antennas. In embedded systems, ESP series controllers from Espressif are popular for building IoT based Applications. ESP32 and ESP8266 are the most commonly use wifi modules for embedded applications. In terms of using the Wi-Fi protocol for IOT, there are some pros & cons to be considered.

The infrastructure or device cost for Wi-Fi is low & deployment is easy but the power consumption is high and the Wi-Fi range is quite moderate. So, the Wi-Fi may not be the best choice for all types of IOT applications but it can be used for applications like Home Automation. There are many development boards available that allow people to build IOT applications using Wi-Fi. The most popular ones are the Raspberry Pi and Node MCU. These boards allow people to build IOT prototypes and also can be used for small real-time applications. Likewise, is the Marvell Avastar 88W8997 SoC, which follows the Wi-Fi's IEEE 802.11n standard. The chip has applications like wearables, wireless audio & smart home.

Bluetooth

Bluetooth

Bluetooth is a technology used for exchanging data wirelessly over short distances and preferred over various IOT network protocols. It uses short-wavelength UHF radio waves of frequency ranging from 2.4 to 2.485 GHz in the ISM band. The Bluetooth technology has 3 different versions based on its applications:

Bluetooth: The Bluetooth that is used in devices for communication has many applications in IOT/M2M devices nowadays. It is a technology using which two devices can communicate and share data wirelessly. It operates at 2.4GHz ISM band and the data is split in packets before sending and then is shared using any one of the designated 79 channels operating at 1 MHz of bandwidth.

BLE (Bluetooth 4.0, Bluetooth Low Energy): The BLE has a single main difference from Bluetooth that it consumes low power. With that, it makes the product of low cost & more long-lasting than Bluetooth.

iBeacon: It is a simplified communication technique used by Apple and is completely based on Bluetooth technology. The Bluetooth 4.0 transmits an ID called UUID for each user and makes it each to communicate between iPhone users.

Bluetooth has many applications, such as in telephones, tablets, media players, robotics systems, etc. The range of Bluetooth technology is between 50 – 150 meters and the data is being shared at a maximum data rate of 1 Mbps.

After launching the BLE protocol, there have been many new applications developed using Bluetooth in the field of IOT. They fall under the category of low-cost consumer products and Smart-Building applications.

Like Wi-Fi, Bluetooth also has a module Bluetooth HC-05 that can be interfaced with development boards like Arduino or Raspberry Pi to build DIY projects. When it comes to Real-time applications, Marvell's Avastar 88W8977 comes with Bluetooth v4.2 and has features like high speed, mesh networking for IOT. Another product, M5600 is a wireless pressure transducer with a Bluetooth v4.0 embedded in it.

Zigbee

ZigBee is another IoT wireless protocols has features similar to the Bluetooth technology. But it follows the IEEE 802.15.4 standard and is a high-level communication protocol. It has some advantages similar to Bluetooth i.e., low-power consumption, robustness, high security, and high scalability.

Zigbee

Zigbee offers a range of about 10 – 100 meters maximum and data rate to transfer data between communicated devices is around 250 Kbps. It has a large number of applications in technologies like M2M & IOT. Having limitations in regards to data rate, range, and power consumption, Zigbee is only appropriate for Small-Scale Wireless applications. Though having some limitations, it provides a 128-bit AES encryption and is giving a big hand in making secure communication for home automation & small Industrial applications. Zigbee too has its DIY module named XBee & XBee Pro which can be interfaced with Arduino or Raspberry Pi boards to make simple projects or application prototypes. The company Develco has made products using Zigbee technologies like Sensors, gateways, meter interfaces, smart plugs, smart relays, etc which all work on the Zigbee wireless Mesh network, consuming low power and free from external interferences. Another company, Data net has Zigbee based products which are used in real-time applications already, like the DNL910 & DNL920.

Z-Wave

Z-Wave is a communication protocol specially designed for Home Automation products and it is also known as a low-power RF communications technology. The data packets are exchanged at data rates of 100kbps maximum and the protocol operates at a frequency of 900 MHz in the ISM band. It has a distance range of up to 30 meters maximum. It supports control of up to 232 devices. The only maker of chips for this technology is Sigma Designs.

Z-Wave

The Z-Wave has module ZIY (Z-Wave It Yourself) which is an Arduino & Raspberry Pi compatible board and can be used for Home Automation applications. Silicon Labs has a product Z-Wave 700, **specially developed for Smart Home applications having features like long battery life** (10 years) and improved range to about 100 meters. Also, the company has launched a Z-Wave 700 Development Kit which includes Z-Wave software, sample code and the module with an adapter, enabling others to develop Z-Wave based application products.

6LoWPAN

6LowPAN (IPv6 Low-power Wireless Personal Area Network) is a network protocol that supports data encapsulation and header compression mechanisms with other applications like that of Bluetooth & ZigBee. The standard can be used across multiple communications platforms, including Ethernet, Wi-Fi, IEEE 802.15.4 and sub-1GHz ISM.

It can be adapted as Bluetooth 4.0 or ZigBee and operate at 2.4 GHz or 900 MHz, respectively. It consumes low power and can be used in a wide number of IOT and M2M applications.

6LoWPAN protocol has a 6LoWPAN L-Tek Arduino Shield that can be connected with Arduino board to get 6LoWPAN connectivity at a frequency band of 900 MHz. The users can **develop application prototypes using the module**. Talking about modules, Melange Systems has Tarang UT20 & TarangMini SM modules that have the connectivity to 6LoWPAN protocol. Microchip has developed SmartConnect 6LoWPAN for IP mesh connectivity over 802.15.4 links in 2.4GHz frequency band. IDT has ZWIR45xx series modules that are used for 6LoWPAN protocol applications.

RFID

Radio-frequency identification (RFID) is a technology that uses electromagnetic fields to identify objects or tags which contains some stored information. The range of RFID varies from about 10cm to 200m maximum and such a long difference makes the two range have names like short-range distance and long-range distance. Since the range has a huge difference, the frequency at which the RFID operates has a huge difference too i.e., it starts from KHz and ranges till GHz or can be said as frequency ranges from Low frequency (LF) to Microwave depending upon the application and distance of communication.

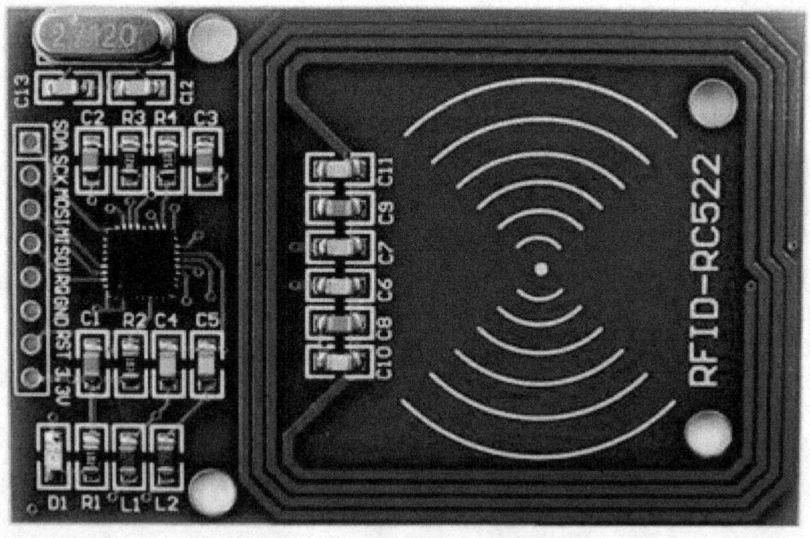

RFID

RFID has RC522 Arduino & Raspberry Pi compatible module that can be used to build an IOT based RFID application or application prototypes like attendace system.

Cellular

The cellular network has been in use since the last 2 decades and comprises of GSM/GPRS/EDGE(2G)/UMTS or HSPA(3G)/LTE(4G) communication protocols. This protocol is generally used **for long-distance communications**. The data can be sent of large size and with high speeds compared to other technologies.

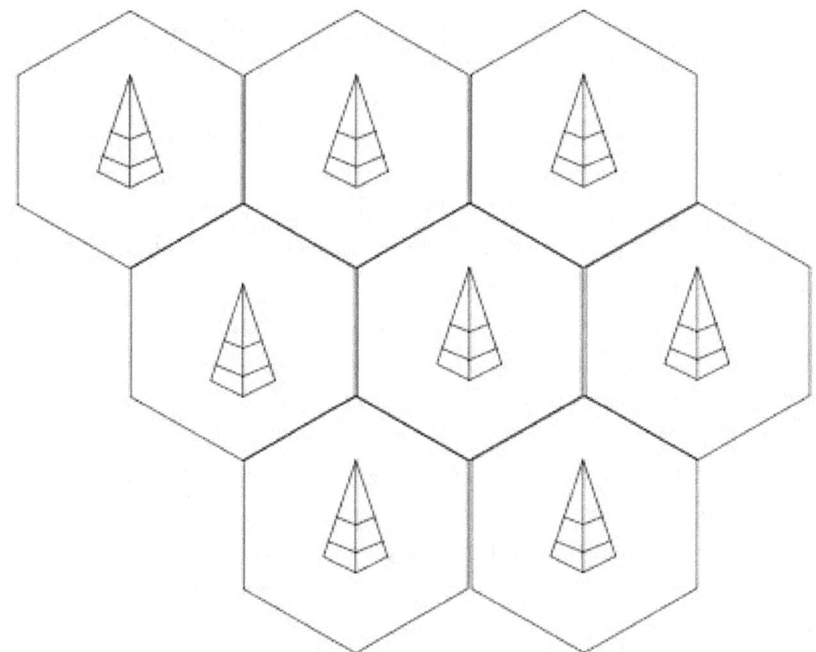

CELLULAR NETWORK

The operating frequencies range from 900 – 2100 MHz with a distance coverage of 35km to 200km and the data rates i.e. the speed of transferring data is from 35 Kbps to 10 Mbps. A company Quectel has cellular IOT products like EC21, EC23, EG91 and many more LTE standard products working on 4G. UMTS/HSPDA UC15, UC20, UC15 Mini & UC20 Mini are the 3G based IOT module launched by the same company.

NB-IOT

NB-IOT stands for **Narrow Band Internet of Things**, is an LPWAN i.e. Low Power Wide Area Network technology. The technology can be used for applications requiring low power consumption, long-distance communication and for a long time (large battery life). The advantage of NB-IOT is that it has good coverage capacity i.e., the signal can transmit through walls or in underground areas where normal cellular signals won't reach. It has a distance coverage of around 10 Kms maximum.

Quectel has launched NB-IOT modules like LTE BC95, LTE BC68 and many more modules that can be used to build real-time products in the field of IOT.

5G

5G is the fifth generation of cellular network protocol. It's designed for high speeds communication between smartphones as well as other devices (unlike the other cellular networks). The download speed is expected to be around 1Gbps on average. The technology protocol will work alongside with 3G & 4G technologies and would have a huge rise in Internet of Things (IOT) technology. The technology has launched in 2019 for test purposes and is available only in a few cities of the world but it is planned to launch worldwide in 2020.

Like having modules for 2G, 3G & 4G, Quectel company also has modules for 5G which are RG500Q and RM500Q, working on a sub-6 GHz frequency band and can be used for building products for IOT.

NFC

NFC (Near Field Communication) is a protocol used for enabling simple and safe two-way interactions between electronic devices. It has mostly smartphones-based applications like allowing contactless payment transactions, accessing digital content and connecting various electronic devices.

NFC

It operates at a frequency of 13.56MHz in the ISM band and the maximum distance range is about 10cm with a data rate of 100–420kbps. It replaces the card swiping payment transaction and can be used for wireless payment like some magic.

Being a good protocol for IOT technology, there are various modules and real-time products that follow the NFC protocol. Like the Seed Studio NFC shield, DFRobot NFC module, Grove NFC, and all 3 of them are Arduino and Raspberry Pi compatible. For real-time products, NFC has CLRC663 plus, MFRC630, NTAG I2C plus products.

LoRaWAN

LoRa is getting popular now days and used in IOT network protocol. LoRaWAN (Long Range Wide Area Network) has applications for long distances and is designed to provide low-power for communication in IoT, M2M applications. It has a capacity of connecting millions of devices with data rates ranging from 0.3 kbps to 50 kbps. The distance for LoRaWAN application ranges from 2 - 5km for the urban environment & maximum 15km for the suburban environment.

LoRaWAN

TE has launched products like MS8607, HTU21D, and MS5637 which are used to get humidity, temperature & barometric pressure values using the LoRaWAN protocol and has a major role in the field of IOT.

LTE-M

LTE-M is also known as LTE (Long Term Evolution) Cat-M1 protocol. It is a technology used to connect IOT devices directly with 4G network without the need to access through any gateway in between. It provides a data rate of about 100 Kbps and chips are less costly. Since it transmits less data, it provides a long battery life to the devices.

A module named LTE BG96 Cat M1 module is used to make IOT based products working on LTE-M protocol. The same module also supports LTE Cat NB1 protocol with an improved data rate of 375 kbps downlink & uplink speed.

So, these are main **communication protocols in IoT** used for developing IoT based applications.

CHAPTER FIVE

DATA STORAGE AND ANALYSIS

The Internet of Things means different things to different people.

To vendors, it's the latest in a slew of large-scale trends to affect their enterprise customers, and the latest marketing bandwagon they have to consider.

To enterprise organizations, it's still a jumble of technical standards, conflicting opinions and big potential. For developers, it's a big opportunity to put together the right mix of tools and technologies, and probably something they are already doing under another name.

Understanding how these technologies work together on a technical level is becoming important, and will provide more opportunities to use software design as part of the overall business.

As Internet of Things projects go from concepts to reality, one of the biggest challenges is

how the data created by devices will flow through the system.

How many devices will be creating information?

How will they send that information back?

Will you be capturing that data in real time, or in batches?

What role will analytics play in future?

IoT refers to a broad network of physical devices that include sensors, vehicles, mobile devices and even home appliances that create and share data.

For enterprises this can mean cameras that monitor footfall, servers that run plant machinery, data collected from remote/branch offices or any location in which the business operates.

The breadth of options for IoT means that almost any device outside the datacentre that generates useful information could be part of an IoT solution.

Typically, IoT devices are seen as individual, remotely managed and embedded appliances such as cameras, but this isn't always the case. Many businesses have distributed environments that run one or more servers at branch locations to monitor building access, environmental controls or other tasks that relate directly to the business itself.

As a result, IoT is a mesh of devices that could create, store and process content across many physical locations.

Distributed data and IoT

Probably the most obvious statement here is that the information created is outside the datacentre.

We are increasingly seeing the term "edge" used to describe computing and data management tasks performed outside core datacentres. Although edge computing has existed for many years, the current evolution in IoT and edge computing is notable for the sheer volume of data created in non-core datacentre locations.

This brings unique challenges to IT departments that must ensure this data is adequately secured, collated and processed.

Most IT organisations are used to knowing exactly where their data resides. With IoT, the challenge of putting arms around all of the content owned by a business is much greater, with obvious implications on user privacy and regulations, such as the General Data Protection Regulation (GDPR).

Distributed processing

With the possibility of so much information being created at the edge, it's impossible to move the data into the datacentre for processing in a timely fashion.

First, with a wide variety of devices deployed it may be simply impossible for a business to move the data into the datacentre without investing heavily in external networking.

Second, in many instances the value of the data may not be best served by storing the entire content. For example, a camera that counts cars passing a traffic intersection doesn't need to store the entire video, just report back the number of cars counted over specific time periods. The video data could be moved back at some time in the future or simply discarded.

A third point to consider is the timely processing of data. IoT devices may need to make local processing decisions quickly and not tolerate the latency of reading and writing the data into a core datacentre for processing to occur.

This distributed data and processing requirement means that businesses need to add the capability to push compute and applications to the edge and, in many cases, pre-process data before it is uploaded to the core datacenter for long-term processing.

The IoT information lifecycle

This brings us neatly to the subject of information lifecycle management (ILM).

ILM has been a broad aspiration of IT organisations for more than 30 years. Initially, this meant having the ability to move data between tiers of storage as the content aged and became less valuable. Eventually, data would end up in an archive or on tape.

In the modern enterprise, ILM is much more nuanced than it used to be.

As we've discussed, data is created at the edge and potentially pre-processed by in-situ edge computing devices. Over time, the data can be consolidated into core locations for further processing.

Businesses are increasingly starting to focus on getting additional value from all the data in the organisation by using artificial intelligence (AI) and machine learning (ML) techniques. AI/ML systems require huge quantities of data to train models and develop algorithms that in turn can be pushed back out to the edge as part of the pre-processing of data.

In this sense, ILM doesn't look to directly optimise the cost of storing data, but instead to ensure it can be placed in the right location for the processing needed at the time. We're starting to see the flow of information from the edge into core locations that continue to derive value long after the data was initially created.

IoT and public cloud

IoT data is mostly unstructured and so can easily be stored in public cloud infrastructure.

All the major cloud providers offer low-cost scalable storage systems based on object storage technology. With high-speed networks and no charge for data ingress, public cloud is a great location to store the volumes of IoT data being generated by businesses.

But, public cloud has more to give. Cloud service providers have extended their product offerings to include big data analysis tools that ingest and process large volumes of unstructured content. This allows businesses to create highly scalable ML/AI applications to process data potentially more efficiently than could be achieved in a private datacenter.

Supplier solutions in IoT

Looking at what suppliers are developing; we see a range of products and solutions. Here are some examples of how the requirements of IoT and storage are being addressed.

Some startup companies are developing in-situ processing storage devices that allow data to be analysed at the edge.

NGD Systems, for example, offers a range of "computational storage" products that look like traditional NVMe SSDs, but that also allow application code to run within the drive.

Meanwhile, ScaleFlux offers similar technology that can offload common tasks (such as erasure coding, database acceleration) to the storage device.

Amazon Web Services (AWS) provides the capability to import edge data into AWS S3 using Snowball. A Snowball appliance is effectively a ruggedised server with storage that can be used to physically transport data from an offsite location. AWS has further extended the capability of Snowball with Snowball Edge, which allows local data processing either with EC2 instances or Lambda functions.

Pure Storage, NetApp and DDN have all developed converged infrastructure or hardware reference architectures to use storage to support on-premise ML/AI systems. In these instances, the storage hardware provides the ability to process large volumes of data in parallel at extremely low latency.

Microsoftis working on project Brainwave, custom hardware to process data in real time as it is ingested from external sources. This is driving a move towards real-time AI processing.

Google already offers services in Google Cloud Platform (GCP) to process large data sets and is now looking at addressing the technology towards industry verticals. Still in early access development, Google is working on custom ASIC hardware that can be deployed at the edge to do initial ML/AI data processing.

Storage software startups such as WekaIO, E8 Storage and Excelero have developed products that provide scalable file and block storage for low latency analytics requirements. In the case of WekaIO, the software can also be installed on the public cloud (AWS) to create a highly scalable storage platform that uses NVMe storage.

StorMagic, a UK-based company, provides the capability to deploy scalable and resilient storage at the edge using SvSAN. The company has thousands of deployments of SvSAN running on standard hypervisors at edge locations such as wind farms and retail outlets.

HCP from Hitachi Vantara can be used as a centralised object store and archive for IoT data. Tools such as Hitachi's Pentaho platform then visualise this data, making it easier to build data pipelines for use by the business to create value from disparate content stores.

IoT challenges

What becomes obvious when looking at the range of storage solutions on offer is the lack of standardisation in the market today.

There are no clear best practices or industry standards to ensure distributed data is securely accessed and transported into core datacentres. Data is typically moved in an asynchronous fashion, which risks it becoming inconsistent or out of step with copies in the datacentre.

As we move forward, the challenge for data storage and data management companies is to develop standards and tools that treat data outside the datacentre with the same level of security and consistency as within our public and private clouds.

IoT Edge Computing – Types, Architecture, Advantages & Applications:

Today IoT edge computing is defining the future of IoT (Internet of things). It is imparting stability to the IoT devices and addressing latency issues by providing data processing closer to the source. Leveraging the power of cloud, IoT has grown exponentially and has been installing several billion smart devices in the IoT network every year.

Such a vast network is now demanding for high capacity data processing techniques. Data scientists and data analysts are facing major challenges in data analysis, especially where data processing needs to be done in real time. This problem is now being handled by IoT Edge Computing Technology.

What is IoT Edge Computing

International Data Corporation (IDC) has defined IoT Edge Computing as a network of small data centers where critical data is stored and processed locally. These data centers are connected in the form of a mesh and they push the data received to a centrally located storage repository. This is typically within a span of 100 sq ft or less.

IoT Edge Computing is used for data analysis and processing closer to the data source. Smart devices used in IoT Edge Computing are capable of processing critical data fragments and provide a quick real time response. These devices prevent the delay caused by sending the data through internet to cloud and linger for cloud response.

These devices are designed to act as tiny data centers that provide nearly zero latency. With this enhanced capability, data processing is decentralized and network traffic is greatly reduced. This data can later be collected by the cloud for further evaluation and processing.

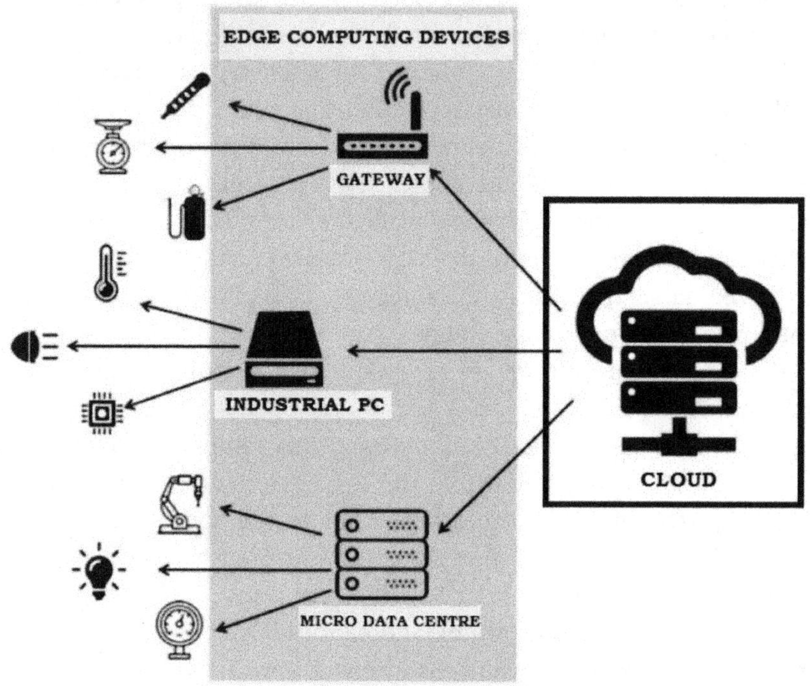

EDGE COMPUTING

Types of IoT Edge Computing

- Local devices for accommodating a specific and well-defined purpose. These can be easily deployed and maintained.
- Local data centers for providing significant processing and storage capacities. These are generally pre- engineered and customized. They are assembled onsite and provide for good capital expenditure savings.
- Regionally located data centers that have a distinct advantage of being closer to the source of data. While they have greater processing and

storage power than local data centers, they are expensive and require more maintenance. Such edge devices are designed either with prefabricated or made-to-order variants.

Architecture of IoT Edge Computing

Due to the advantages of power, cost and space, conventional analytical clusters do not support edge computing. The power, cooling, space and such other functional costs make these clusters expensive. They also do not offer the simplicity or speed that is necessary for the feasibility of edge computing.

Businesses have now gone beyond the x86 clustered architectures that have hindered real time analytical innovation. They are seeking accelerated systems that provide the size, performance and required speed.

These new systems are using hybrid technologies that integrate various computing technologies like x86, FPGA or GPU. They are compact, require little power and yet provide high performance that surpass today's conventional systems.

In scenarios where there is a scarcity of resources, these versatile systems complement incumbent infrastructure and improve the performance of the existing clusters.

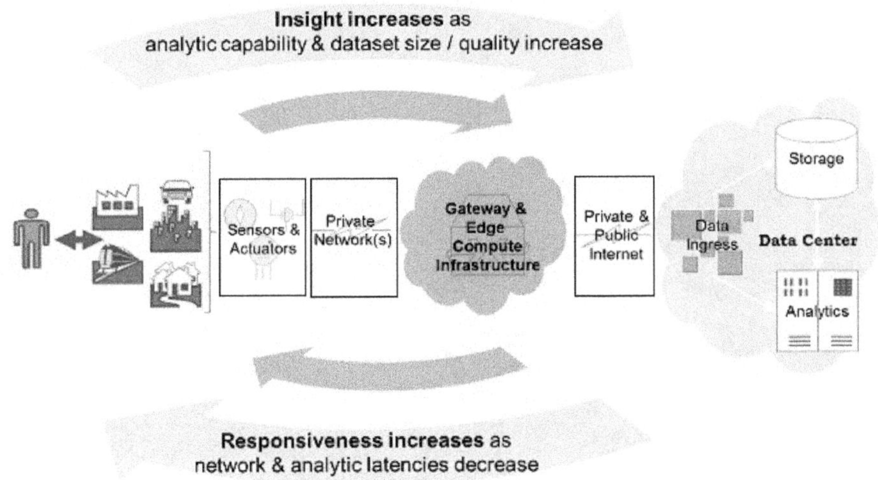

ARCHITECTURE OF EDGE COMPUTING

Advantages of IoT Edge Computing

As IoT Edge Computing is being adopted and taken mainstream, large number of industries are reaping its potential advantages. Edge computing, particularly, brings in seven major advantages in smart manufacturing.

1. Quicker Response Time

Power of computation and data storage is local and distributed. Avoiding a cloud round trip is key for reducing latency and facilitates faster responses. This will assist in preventing the breaking down of vital machine operations or the occurrence of hazardous incidents.

2. Consistent Operations with Sporadic Connectivity

For many remote assets, supervising unpredictable internet connectivity areas like farm pumps, oil wells, windmills or solar farms can be challenging. Edge devices' capability for local storage and data processing ensures that no data is lost and prevents operational failures in case of limited internet connection.

3. Security

IoT Edge Computing has made the transfer of data between the cloud and devices redundant. It is now possible to filter sensitive data locally and transmit only the data model over to the cloud.

This allows the user to build a satisfactory security framework that is necessary for enterprise audits and security.

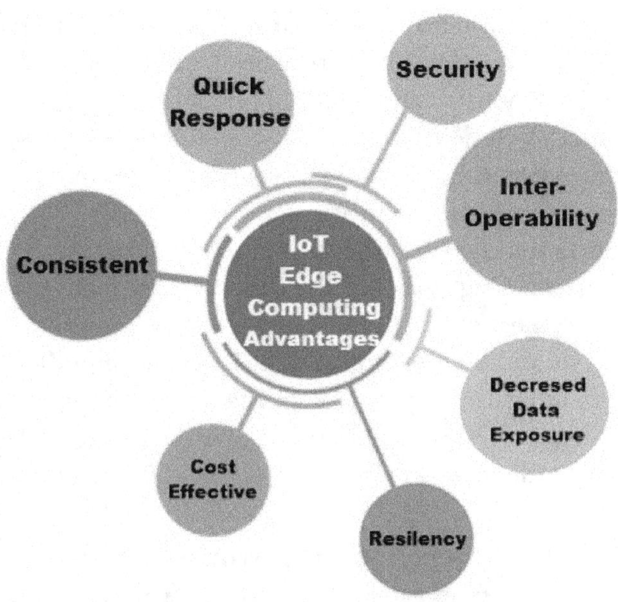

SECURITY

4. Cost Effective Solution

A major practical concern while adopting IoT was the cost incurred due to data storage, computational power and network bandwidth.

IoT Edge computing enables local data computations that allow business establishments to distinguish between services that have to be run locally and those that must be sent to cloud. This helps in reducing the closing costs of establishing a complete IoT solution.

5. Interoperability between Modern and Legacy Devices

Edge devices function as a communication link between contemporary and legacy machines. This provides the legacy machines to interact with modern devices for IoT solutions.

6. Increased Resiliency

Decentralized architecture of edge computing enables the other network devices to become resilient to a greater extent. This is a great virtue since a single machine failing on the cloud would mean thousands of IoT devices getting affected.

Failure of one device on edge will not affect other network devices.

7. Decreased Data Exposure

As we know, edge computing minimizes data transfer through the network. This in turn helps reduce data exposure during transit. In few cases, sensitive information like Personally Identifiable Information (PII) and Payment Card Industry (PCI) may not be sent at all.

Such instances will help in avoiding several legal, security and privacy complications. Further, data encryption and access control can make it highly secure against familiar threats.

IoT Edge Computing Applications

IoT Edge Computing is being used in various applications. We will discuss two of its most popular use cases here.

Data Analysis and Monitoring using IoT Edge Computing Sensors

IoT sensors are gathering large data that is set to grow exponentially every year. Using IoT Edge Computing allows businesses to simplify and speed up the analytics and get the right insights at the right time.

Data Analysis and Monitoring using IoT Edge Computing Sensors

Thinning Mobile Data using IoT Edge Computing

Like IoT data, mobile data is also being created rapidly. However, the drawback of such massive data is that not all but only a selective part of it is required for queries related to data analysis.

IoT Edge Computing enables better understanding of data and help process only information that is essential to the query.

Identifying outliers and anomalies

Internet of Things (IoT) is the integration of physical objects which are attached with electronics, software, sensors, and network connectivity, that allow them to capture and transmit data. In IoT, a thing refers to a physical object that includes sensors to communicate with the real world through a network to perform certain functions. Things can include smart phones, tablets, cameras, fridges, watches, televisions, etc. IoT is considered a great advancement in the area of information technology. IoT is a network system which links various communication devices with the internet to reach quick, reliable and real-time information exchange and communication that help in intelligent management. As a result, objects can be monitored remotely allowing for the communication between the physical and virtual worlds. The evolution of the IoT paradigm depends substantially on current technologies internet, mobile technologies, cloud computing, communication protocols and embedded sensors to capture the data. Through the IoT technology, real world objects situated around people in their surrounding environment are linked with each other, also these objects have internet connectivity to exchange data then take appropriate actions correspondingly. The objects capture data about the surrounding environment to monitor certain phenomena such as temperature and humidity. In IoT, data is generated by things, not by people as in the case of the internet such as data generated by social networks. The networking of devices will generate huge amounts of data that need media to get stored. Real world objects are the main components of the IoT paradigm, each object has a unique identity and can access the network to integrate the physical and digital worlds to offer enhanced capabilities to people. Recently, small sized devices with huge enhancements in processing power and storage are suitable for embedding sensors to them. The integration between those devices and sensors can offer great capabilities to users. The IoT can offer device to device, device to people and device to environment information transmission through the incorporation of information space and physical space. IoT allows for information exchange between things and things or between people and things.

The main characteristics of IoT are: comprehensive perception, reliable transmission and intelligent processing, described as follows:

1. **Comprehensive perception:** sensors capture data anytime and anywhere by utilizing the perception, acquisition and measurement technology using Radiofrequency Identification (RFID). Perception is concerned with monitoring real world phenomena or events.

2. **Reliable transmission:** allows objects to interact with networks and achieve robust information exchange anytime through using a variety of communication technologies and communication networks.

3. **Intelligent processing:** analyzes the enormous quantities of sensors' data through using various intelligent computing technologies to aid the decision-making process.

Huge data amounts are generated through IoT applications. Data in IoT is characterized by the 5V model:

1. **V**olume: enormous amounts of generated data.

2. **V**ariety: various data types such as structured, semi-structured and unstructured data.

3. **V**elocity: high speed of data generation and processing.

4. **V**eracity: accuracy and trustworthiness of the generated data. 5. **V**alue: benefits gained from using the data.

High usage of smart phones and internet connectivity led to the increase of many sensor-based applications. IoT has several applications in various fields such as healthcare, agriculture, smart homes, transportation, education, economics and business.

IoT applications will be embedded in people's daily lives to offer smart capabilities to make their lives easier, more convenient and intelligent.

IoT applications are divided into three main categories:

1. **Personal:** such as smart homes, healthcare systems and wearables. For example, a smart home application could be the automatic adjustment of the light based on people's availability in a certain room. Also, a healthcare application can monitor the amount of calories taken by a person and send him/her an alert when the amount of calories increases above a certain threshold. Moreover, currently there are various watches and glasses that monitor the heartbeat of people then notifications are sent to people when the heartbeat reaches a certain value.

2. **Social:** such as traffic management and environment management. Traffic management through IoT can be very useful to monitor the traffic patterns of the city and take accordingly the corresponding actions. Regarding environment management applications, they are numerous, one application is monitoring the pollution level in a certain city to help in the

decision-making process by the authorities.

3. **Business:** such as automation of supply chain and retail.

IoT faces a lot of obstacles ranging from data capturing and management to security threats. IoT comprises a lot of security threats as millions of devices are connected to exchange data. In addition, data interoperability in IoT is crucial because sensors generate massive amounts of data with various formats. Also, data fusion techniques are needed to integrate data of various formats generated from different sensors' types. Moreover, the IoT paradigm is susceptible to a high noise rate since it depends mainly on sensors which may be of low power and poor quality. IoT is still in its beginning so it faces a lot of challenges to have successful implementation of various IoT applications. One great challenge is the detection of data anomalies coming out from sensors' data. An anomaly/outlier is a data point that varies substantially from the remaining data points, as though it was produced by another technique. Detecting anomalies are useful because they are doubtful of not being produced by the same methods as the other data points.

Detection of data anomalies in the IoT paradigm is a complicated task because it is difficult to define the normal pattern of data as data in IoT is domain dependent.

Also, data comes from heterogeneous sensors with various formats. The data involved in the IoT environment is usually time series data or streaming data as sensors generate time stamped data continuously with great amounts. Time series data refers to a sequence of data values captured in time order, usually captured at equal intervals, while data stream refers to unbounded series of data generated continuously by data sources.

CATEGORIES OF ANOMALIES

Anomalies are categorized into three types described as follows:

1. **Global/point anomaly:** in a particular data set, a data point is a global anomaly if it differs greatly from the remaining data points. As a result, a suitable assessment of divergence is needed to differentiate between normal points and anomalies. This type of anomalies is considered the easiest category of anomalies to detect and the majority of anomaly detection methods focus on detecting it. There are various applications for global anomaly detection such as intrusion detection and trading transactions auditing systems.

2. **Contextual anomaly:** in a specific data set, a data point is considered a contextual outlier if it noticeably varies in the defined context. Contextual

anomalies are also denoted as conditional anomalies because they depend on a specific context. As a result, to detect contextual anomalies, the context has to be defined as a component of the problem definition.

In contextual anomaly detection, the attributes of the data objects in consideration are classified into two categories:

• Contextual attributes: these features define the object's context. Context can refer to time or location.

• Behavioral attributes: these attributes denote the object's characteristics, and are used to assess whether the data point is an anomaly in the context to which it is situated at.

3. **Collective anomaly**: in a certain data set, a subset of data objects creates a collective anomaly if the objects as a whole differ greatly from the whole data set. The individual data objects may not be outliers. Collective anomaly detection has several applications. For example, stock transaction among two parties is considered normal, but a big collection of transactions of the same stock between a small party in a short duration is a collective anomaly as it may be an indication of some people tampering the market.

Unlike global or contextual anomaly detection, in collective anomaly detection we have to take into account both the behavior of the individual objects and the groups of objects. Consequently, background knowledge of the relationship between the data objects such as distance or similarity measurement is essential to discover collective anomalies.

Anomaly Detection in IoT

Since IoT is in its early beginning, little work explored the detection of anomalies in the IoT environment. A proposed technique is used to detect data anomalies utilizing expert knowledge. A prototype for anomaly detection was implemented using Raspberry Pi to track anomalies in data generated from sensors in an IoT environment. The approach was simulated on a smart home. Tracking procedure of anomalies was implemented through verifying the generated data values from sensors across some conditions. The proposed technique made use of expert knowledge and the possible anticipated attacks for detecting anomalies through a list of predefined constraints on the data.

The constraints were related to either of the following:

time flow, business logic, technical conditions, whole system structure and prior sensor's values.

In a real-world simulation prototype was presented that made use of IoT smart objects to discover behavioral-based anomalies across a simulated smart home. Through the simulation environment, the smart home and the surrounding world were tracked with a **behavioral modeling intrusion detectionsystem** (BMIDS).

The BMIDS employed immunity inspired algorithms to differentiate between normal and abnormal behavioral patterns. The proposed simulation process observed all relevant activities to build precise behavioral models. The BMIDS represented IoT sensor data as a list of event sequences along with the simulated world states to construct a numerical illustration for behavioral identity. In an unsupervised anomaly detection technique employing light switches was presented. The proposed approach utilized a statistical-based algorithm using expectation maximization to build the mixture models. Through the proposed technique, an anomaly was correlated with a probability. Gaussian mixture models with the same-shape constraint were utilized to prevent the occurrence of high variances. This technique was tested in a real apartment having three people. In an outlier detection approach using Hadoop framework and Mahout K-means algorithm was presented.

Hadoop is a software framework that allows for distributed processing of big data using MapReduce.

MapReduce is a programming model for big data processing through a parallel distributed algorithm on clusters.

Mahout is an open-source machine learning library provided by Apache.

K-means algorithm is a type of clustering techniques which depends on a similarity measure among objects.

To make use of the proposed algorithm, the LinkSmart Internet of Things middleware, implemented in the Hydra Project by adding a new module in the middleware. In a correlation-based anomaly detection technique was proposed as a predictive maintenance approach for compact electric generators. Correlations between sensors were chosen by using statistical analysis and anomalies were discovered through utilizing both sensor data and correlation coefficients between sensors. In a novel concept of urban heartbeat which was built using data from sensors in the environment was presented. Urban Heartbeat gathered the contextual information about patterns which occur frequently in the environment. Techniques were developed to find couplings between sensors. After that, quasiperiodic patterns from the time series data were discovered. The urban heartbeat can be used to discover unexpected events that deviate significantly from the normal behavior. In a case study of smart environment based on real time data captured by the city of Aarhus, Denmark was presented.

Various air pollution elements were used to find the unhealthy or anomalous locations.

Anomalies were detected through analyzing the air quality index, which is a numerical measure used to discover the anomalous locations in the city, which exceed certain threshold in order to have healthy atmosphere. Neural networks, neuro-fuzzy method and support vector machines for both binary and multi class problems were used to detect anomalous locations from a pollution database. An IoT rules generation and execution framework which consists of three parts, a machine learning rule discovery, a threat prediction model builder and tools to guarantee quick reaction to rules violation and variations in traffic behavior of sensors' data. Random-Forest with some proposed enhancements was used for rules generation and anomaly detection. The proposed enhancements were: presenting a selection criterion for eliminating the redundant trees to minimize the run time, introducing the concept of prioritizing trees by their probability of reaching the correct decision instead of removing them and utilizing Message Queue Telemetry Transport (MQTT) protocol, which is a lightweight messaging protocol over Transmission Control Protocol (TCP) in the framework since it is adapted to the IoT environment.

Anomaly Detection in Time Series Data

Various techniques were applied on time series data to detect anomalies. They will be presented by categories in the following subsections.

Statistical Approaches

A lot of work was done in data anomaly detection for time series data using statistical approaches. In a two-stage technique to detect anomalies in natural gas consumption levels time series data was proposed. The proposed technique was able to discover different types of anomalies found in the natural gas field. A linear regression model was deduced from the natural gas field and a geometric probability distribution of the residuals was constructed, to calculate the probability of a data value being outlier. The residuals are the discrepancies between the actual and calculated values. In the next phase, a Bayesian maximum likelihood classifier was trained depending on the various anomalies discovered in the previous phase. The extrema of the residuals were analyzed to discover anomalies. An extremum is considered an anomaly if its probability of existing in the same distribution as the rest of data points in the residual set is lower than the probability of satisfying a type I error at a certain level of significance. A customized method for discovering unusual sleep by utilizing personal differences among people was implemented. The unusual sleep refers to the statistical anomalies in the sleep time series data.

The technique was implemented through two steps: dimension reduction through permutation entropy and outlier detection. Two approaches for detecting unusual sleep were presented.

The first approach was the S_n estimator which is a deviation-based method for discovering global anomalies.

The second approach was Local Outlier Factor which is a density-based method for identifying local outliers.

Autoregressive and Moving Average Model (ARMA) was used. An approach for identifying anomalies in scientific workflows and applications working on networked clouds was presented. The presented technique utilized regression based statistical methods to provide model parameters to fit the data.

The errors were calculated using the estimated and actual values, then anomaly notifications were created when the error increased above a specific threshold.

Two approaches were presented for the anomaly detection process: moving average and autoregression. Moving average is a technique which shows the trend of the data set through calculating the average of subsets of data points. The autoregression model captured the previous data values to calculate the next value. An adaptive real-time technique based on auto regression and moving average model was presented for radar's health series data.

Three various techniques for outlier detection were implemented:

1. **Autoregressive integrated moving average:** autoregressive means that a certain data value depends on its previous values at preceding time points. The moving average component of the model defines that the forecast error at time point can be described by past forecast errors at previous time points.
2. **Median absolute deviation scale estimate:** constructed a moving window of length k centered at every data value, then the median of the window and the median absolute deviation were measured.
3. **Rosner statistics:** the technique discovered the k extreme studentized deviates (ESD statistic). After that the highest deviant outlier was

extracted and the approach recalculated the ESD values for the rest of k -1 points. The technique was repeated to measure the ESD values for the rest of data till all k points were computed.

For the three discussed techniques, statistical measures related to the models were calculated and thresholds were set to discover the anomalies.

Neural Networks

neural networks were used for detecting anomalies. A novel algorithm was presented which utilized the wavelets, neural networks and Hilbert transform to detect anomalies. The wavelets were used to remove noise from the original signal. Next, a nonlinear autoregressive neural network was trained to simulate the output signal in the ordinary environment. After that, the error signal which is the discrepancy between the neural network's output and the de-noised signal, was processed through the Hilbert transform. Then the outcome of the analysis was employed to detect anomalies. Recurrent neural networks were used to find out anomalies in flight data. Recurrent neural networks with long short term memory cells and recurrent neural networks with gated recurrent units were used to analyze multivariate sequential time-series data, without the need for dimensionality reduction techniques, and were capable in discovering outliers in latent features. Recurrent neural networks vary from traditional neural networks in permitting the output of hidden layer neurons to feedback and act as inputs to the neurons. As a result, the network was capable to use previous readings to analyze the time series data. Autoregressive with exogenous inputs and artificial neural network models were employed to capture the features of time series data. Anomalies were observed by using hypothesis testing on the extrema of the residuals. The proposed approach was capable in differentiating between anomalies and data values in the tails of the residual distribution, through considering the statistics of the residuals and the quantity of samples in the data set.

Clustering

Clustering techniques were used for outlier detection. An anomaly detection technique of soft sensor modeling of time series data was proposed.

The technique worked as follows:

it divided the data into segments, after that it detected anomalies for each segment with Density-based spatial clustering of applications with noise (DBSCAN) algorithm. DBSCAN puts high density areas into a cluster which is considered the biggest set of connected points. The proposed algorithm integrated the DBSCAN algorithm with soft sensor modeling process. The training errors and testing errors were utilized to aid in setting the parameters (epsilon and minimum points) for the DBSCAN algorithm. Epsilon refers to the neighborhood radius and minimum points define the minimum number of available objects.

Next, the data sets were filled using the moving average after removing the anomalies. Then, a soft sensor model was constructed with new data sets, and the modeling errors were employed into the outlier detection algorithm. An outlier detection method was presented to find out anomalies on the basis of volume series of high frequency tick-by tick data of stock market. At first the data was pre-processed, then the high frequency data was converted to a ratio matrix and then fed into the outlier detection method to find anomalies. K-means clustering was used Dina ElMenshawy and Waleed Helmy in the anomaly detection process. Also, thresholds were used to detect anomalies through processing the ratio matrix.

Other Techniques

A hierarchical temporal memory (HTM) to time-series based anomaly detection technique was presented. HTM is a new biological neural network that simulates the architecture and functions of the neocortex. It offers great capabilities in continuously learning data patterns.

HTM worked as follows:

it learns by analyzing patterns and the relations between patterns. Then, new patterns were loaded instead of old patterns and predictions were made depending on the stored patterns. When a new data value comes, HTM makes prediction based on the available patterns and compares its inference to the new input. After that, a scoring component measured the degree of the input variance from the inferred value to generate an anomaly score. A prediction algorithm for anomaly detection to univariate time series was proposed. The proposed technique was based on the Least Square Support Vector Machine (LS-SVM) to accomplish multi-step prediction. The LS-SVM algorithm is considered an improved technique of the support vector machine algorithm. The major characteristic of LSSVM algorithm is the occurrence of equality constraints instead of the inequality constraints. Consequently, the quadratic programming problems can be transferred into linear equations. The predicted value and the predicted interval were computed which define the normal range of the expected value. After that, the updated value with the expected interval and the predicting model were compared. If the updated value increased above the range interval, it was declared as an anomaly. In the coming section, the characteristics of data streams are presented, then literature review of anomaly detection in data stream is presented by categories.

Data Stream

The data stream is a consecutive endless series of data values having certain features, such as:

• Transient: a certain data value is important for only a certain period of time, and it is no more useful.

• Time stamp: unlike traditional data, data streams have time stamps.

• Infinite: unbounded set of data values.

• Arrival rate: data arrives continuously from data sources.

• Uncertainty: since sometimes sensors are placed in an open environment, so they are susceptible to external events.

• Concept drift: data points in a data stream vary over time as a result of variations in environments and data trends.

Statistical Approaches

A novel algorithm for detecting anomalies was proposed which partitioned the data space into grid cells with bottom-up approach. Next, when data stream arrived, the statistics information of every grid cell was computed and updated if the data values in the grid cell changed. By time, the importance of historical statistics information of each grid cell will diminish. When a certain amount of time elapsed, the statistics information of each grid cell will decay and be modified. Moreover, a decay function of grid cell information was used to adjust the effect of historical data stream information on the detection accuracy, to discover the changes of anomaly and normal data points through time. A KDTree was constructed to index the historical data, KNNS (K nearest Neighbor Search) was done on every data value to detect anomalies and calculated a predicted value. KD-Tree is a special kind of BST (Binary Search Tree), which is utilized to index multi-dimensional data. BST is a binary tree which satisfies certain conditions: each node n consisted of a left sub-tree, right sub-tree and an element, also no duplicate nodes exist in BST and there is a specific route from the root node to any point in the same BST. A value was defined as an anomaly, when the actual measurement from the data stream was deviated substantially from the predicted value. Also, other anomaly detection techniques were used:

• Naive predicting method which used autoregression.

• Median filter method which selected the median in the data window as the expected value for the current measurement.

• Polynomial fitting method which worked as follows: given the data window, using the least squares method, m order polynomial fitting was done to infer the value of the present measurement where the order m was defined by experts. After that, the deviation from the sensor data to the predicted value was computed to detect anomalies.

The presented techniques were:

1. **Value-Range:** specified the normal behavior of a sensor measurement and values that didn't lie within the specified range were considered anomalies.

2. **Relative deviation:** a big deviation between timely near values can be anomalous.

3. **Distribution-Model:** a distribution model can discover anomalies.

4. **Interval analysis:** metadata such as the timestamp of capturing the data can aid in detecting anomalies.

5. **Cohort analysis:** for example: a big number of similar machines need to be checked; these machines are named a cohort. Anomalous machines can be detected by comparing their behavior to the behavior of the entire cohort.

6. **Time series analysis:** analysis of time series data.

A non-parametric streaming data anomaly detection analytic engine for automatic network management system development was proposed. The engine was implemented so that it can be embedded as a part in current network management systems.

Two algorithms were implemented:

1. A forecasting based anomaly detection technique which used a time series forecasting algorithm. Forecasting performs predictions of future values based on historical values. Anomalies were found based on the deviation between the actual and predicted values.

2. A heuristic limits-based anomaly detection technique, the heuristic limits of the incoming actual values were computed based on historical values and they described the expected normal data boundaries.

If the actual values were not within these limits, they were declared as anomalies.

Principal Component Analysis (PCA)

Principal component analysis was used to detect outliers. A novel technique for anomaly prediction using information entropy theory and

PCA theory was proposed.

The technique worked as follows:

at first, a data feature matrix and the corresponding Dina ElMenshawy and Waleed Helmy entropy matrix were created. Entropy is an estimate of the uncertainty of a random variable in information theory. After that, the matrices were analyzed through PCA. PCA is a classical technique for dimension reduction that converts a multidimensional dataset onto a lower dimensional subspace. After that, feature selection was done, the top r components with the greatest amounts of data variance that PCA measured were selected as principal components. Finally, a support vector regression prediction model was trained using the r principal components. The anomalies were discovered by examining the relative errors between the computed values and the equivalent predicted values.

Two power method-based techniques for outlier detection, using **kernel PCA** and **incremental PCA** were proposed. Kernel PCA is a variation of PCA that implements eigen analysis in a feature space which is nonlinear to the input space. The power method was used when only a small number of principal components are required. The incremental Power PCA method was effective in adjusting covariance matrices in an online manner, while the kernel PCA was robust in nonlinearly mapping inputs to a high-dimensional feature space, so it was efficient in differentiating between normal and anomaly data points.

Support Vector Machine (SVM)

An anomaly detection approach based on cost sensitive support vector machine (CSVM) for multi-dimensional data stream was proposed.

At first, a multi-dimensional sequence transforming technique which convert sequences into features vectors was presented.

Next, a feature selection technique was performed to prune unnecessary features. After that, abnormal sequences in data stream were detected using C-SVM, which was implemented as a classification problem containing two classes: normal and anomaly. An online outlier detection approach based on least squares one-class support vector machine classifiers for detecting outliers in a large power grid network was proposed. The one-class (OC) SVM is an unsupervised learning technique, to capture regions in the input space where the majority of the training objects are found. A least squares (LS) approach of the OC SVM defines that the solution can be produced by solving a linear system instead of a quadratic programming problem in the standard OC SVM. Also, the approximate linear dependence criterion to get a sparse representation of the decision hyperplane in LS-OC-SVM. The sparse online LS-OC-SVM discovered the hyperplane that decreases the squared distances to the images of the training points in the feature space. So, the distance from the hyperplane can be utilized as a metric of similarity between a new data value and the training data.

Other Techniques

An approach for discovering anomalies in data streams through detecting minimal infrequent patterns was proposed. A pattern was considered infrequent when its support in the window does not increase above the specified minimum support threshold. A data stream was described as an unbounded series of transactions. The sliding window model was used to analyze only the latest transactions from the data stream. Three different measures were presented to calculate the outlier degree of a transaction. The minimal infrequent patterns were considered outliers.

A novel system was built using Apache Spark was developed. Apache Spark is a general-purpose engine for large scale data processing. Two metrics were used to discover anomalies in high velocity streams and/or huge volumes of data at rest. The first metric was relative entropy which is a non-symmetric measure of information loss, it computes the difference between two probability distributions P and Q. D represents the degree of difference between the two probability distributions. When the value of D increased, anomalies were discovered. The second metric was Pearson correlation coefficient which is a statistical measure that computes the dependence between two variables. Thresholds were set and used with these metrics to detect anomalies.

An algorithm was proposed to detect anomalies based on fuzzy rules. The algorithm worked as follows:

1. The algorithm was initialized with a hypersphere rule, with the middle at the mean of the first two data values.

2. When a new data value arrived, the effective boundaries of each rule were modified utilizing a weighted formula inversely proportional to the Mahalanobis distance of the data value to every rule.

3. If the algorithm found certain number of consecutive anomalies, a new rule was inserted and was initialized using these observations.

4. Finally, the algorithm discovered two kinds of change points: a change leading to a new rule and a change if the active rule in the rule set changed.

An anomaly detection methodology named Denstream for detecting spam tweets in Twitter was proposed. The proposed algorithm was implemented based on DBSCAN clustering algorithm. Denstream algorithm has two parameters: epsilon and minimum points. Denstream algorithm clustered the tweets and defined spam as anomalies.

CHAPTER SIX

MAKING BUILDINGS SMARTER

Calling a building "smart" implies that technology is embedded to make that building more efficient, useful, convenient and profitable. The goal is to program efficiency beyond what humans can provide.

But "smart" also may imply a healthy dose of marketing hype. No one wants to live in a "dumb building," but it's difficult to define what makes a building smart. And while much is happening now to put real intelligence into buildings—a field known as building automation, it remains to be seen how widely that technology is adopted.

"The building automation industry is in a time of transition," said John Ellis, digitalization portfolio manager at Siemens Building Technologies. "The building industry, like so many other industries, is seeking ways to use digital and intelligent infrastructure to optimize business value."

And in some markets, there is certainly good reason to invest in this technology. Various reports forecast a compound annual growth rate ranging from 10% to 13% in the near future, with the building automation market reaching about $100 billion in 2022. Smart buildings also tie into smart city and smart power-grid technologies, with building automation playing an important part in sustainable building and resource management, some of which are built into local building codes.

Companies working on smart building projects are automating the functions of heating, ventilation and air conditioning (HVAC), the physical security of a structure, energy use, location technology, as well as other areas that building owners and their tenants care about. Better networks, increased connectivity and more compute power are making automation projects possible.

Sensors, controllers, and servers are generally the building blocks of building automation systems. The computing systems capture trends in the data generated by the sensors and do analysis.

Simply put, building automation systems are Internet of Things (IoT) projects mixed with control and automation. Sensors that monitor a local condition send the data about the condition via a high-speed network to be processed. The data is then used to initiate a decision and take an action.

Using the cloud to handle all the data processing may be a necessity for some building automation systems.

Another trend involves an industry shift toward open building automation platforms.

The rule of thumb in designing building automation is security, reliability and ease of use for customers, in that order. Or as Aniruddha Deodhar, principal for smart buildings and smart cities in Arm's IoT Services Group, summed it up: Security, interoperability and connectivity abstraction are the three crucial factors about building automation.

Looking for faults and anomalies in the building systems—another trend in building automation—is useful for more than security.

Today, building automation has evolved significantly beyond control systems for HVAC and lighting. While the concept of smart buildings has been around for some time now, with the emergence of IoT and a new generation of intelligent edge devices, "smart" has taken on an entirely new meaning for building automation.

Buildings of all sizes and functions, residential or commercial, are becoming connected smart ecosystems in which systems monitor and maintain much more than climate control and lighting. Intelligent edge devices will do more than just gather point data. They will also aggregate, analyze, and stream data to edge computing where advanced predictive analytic engines will enable new levels of control and security, while significantly improving the overall user experience in the building environment. These new systems will be smarter, self-learning, innovative, and highly sophisticated.

For owner-operators across an array of residential, commercial, and industrial buildings, the cost of adding smart building technologies could range from hundreds of thousands to millions of dollars. For many companies, the price tag is too high, due, in large part to closed, custom, and proprietary building equipment and software that can only be upgraded by the original manufacturer.

Until recently, this has led to a lack of cost-effective solutions that has kept OEMs and system integrators from delivering affordable smart building management systems (BMS) to a market with a great need for them. Often, owners-operators of small-to-medium size building do not have automated access to data in their facilities, making it difficult to realize energy savings, lower maintenance costs, and improve overall asset performance management (APM) for their buildings.

Today, a lower-cost alternative is to instrument a building using IoT technologies, including low-cost sensors, on premise gateways, distributed control systems, and cloud analytics.

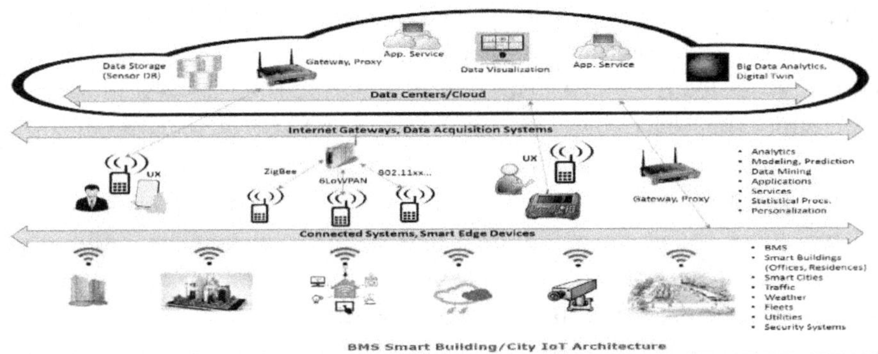

Smart Building

Smart buildings in a perspective of time

Smart buildings, which among others used to be called intelligent buildings, as in intelligent building management (and still are but in recent years there has been a clear change in terminology preference) go back to times Google didn't exist yet.

There are ample so-called ASHRAE transactions, for instance, from the late eighties where you can already find these terms (ASHREA is short for American Society of Heating, Refrigerating and Air-Conditioning Engineers, which de facto is a global organization). Both terms intelligent building and smart building in other words exist since certainly three decades but of course evolved over time.

Just to put that in perspective for younger readers: Google was founded late 1998, you can find back ASHRAE conference proceedings and transactions regarding intelligent buildings since the second half of the eighties and on smart buildings a few years later.

ASHRAE was founded in 1894 by the way but then there was no intelligent or smart building around indeed. The majority of publications with novel approaches in areas such as energy management, HVAC and other areas which still matter in the overall intelligent and smart building perspective really took off in the seventies. It does put things in perspective.

Facility management as a discipline isn't exactly new either. However, here as well many changes, including technological ones, have taken place.

Taking into account the evolutions of the meaning of the terms smart buildings and facility management (it's definitely not primarily about technology), both are increasingly seen in a context of IoT, the integration of IT and OT (Operational Technology), big data analytics, cloud, AI and all these so-called third platform technologies and their several innovation accelerators that drive digital transformation and also change the meaning and face of intelligent and smart buildings, giving direction to their evolutions with equally changing human and societal challenges.

Time for a look at smart buildings and facility management in the scope of real estate, smart cities, the construction industry or AEC industry, and the built environment overall, today and tomorrow.

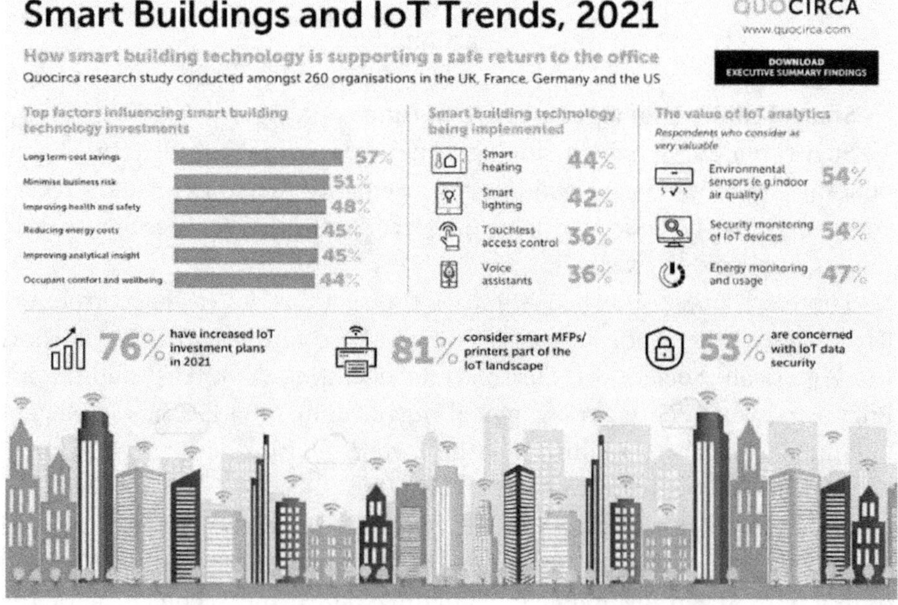

Smart Building IoT trends

Smart facility management in the people, place, process and connected technology perspective of the smart building

Let's start by telling you we love buildings. That's not a joke. Have you ever considered what the possibility to live, work, sleep and whatnot in a building has really meant in the evolution of mankind?

And we mean buildings in the broadest possible sense, including factories, hotels, airports, houses and all the activity that is going on in them. Heating, ventilation, elevators, cooling, security, lighting, an endless list. Most of us are born in a building and spend plenty of key events in our lives in buildings: good moments, bad moments and those extraordinary moments we'll never forget.

How much time do you spend inside buildings? Think about your home, hotels, the places where you work, go to have fun or do business and more. Indeed: a lot!

Even if you exclude the place where you live and call home, you spend ample time in buildings and other facilities. While making your home a safe and agreeable place for you and your loved ones is primarily a matter of your personal preferences, choices and improvements, possibly with the help of experts such as architects or interior designers, one of the many tasks of facility management is to do the same for all the other types of buildings out there.

Smart buildings today: driven by a mix of technologies and evolving demands

We often don't realize it, unless of course we're facility managers, but there are many tasks, processes and efforts going into making the buildings you work in, visit or stay in while traveling, safe, agreeable, efficient (in the sense of ecology, costs and so forth) and, increasingly, 'smart'.

While there is a lot of focus on the smart 'commercial building', the residential smart building, known as the smart home is poised to become a key driver in the Internet of Things (IoT) market as well (it already leads in the main area of IoT investment).

Smart buildings as a cross-industry IoT use case

From that same IoT perspective the smart building space is one of those typical cross-industry markets with tremendous opportunities and evolutions in, among others building management systems, light and room

control **or** critical power **for specific types of buildings** (more about building management in the age of IP and IoT).

With smart buildings, an increasingly important topic in facility management, we are in a far more complex environment than that of the home. At the same time, it's also a far more important one, at least from a broader societal perspective and depending on the function of the building.

While your home is probably much more important to you than, let's say, an office building or a hotel, the impact of all the buildings out there from an energy and ecology perspective alone is huge. This is even more the case if we know that the population in cities is poised to significantly grow, which means more pressure on cities, public buildings and of course a rise of new housing complexes and infrastructural needs. The latter are just some of the many aspects of smart city initiatives and smart cities in evolution overall.

The IoT market in commercial buildings: over $22 Billion in 2026

CHAPTER SEVEN

SMART HEALTH

Internet of Things (IoT) in healthcare

IoT technology brings numerous applications in healthcare, from remote monitoring to smart sensors to medical device integration. It keeps the patients safe and healthy as well as improves the physician delivers care towards the patients.

Healthcare devices collect diverse data from a large set of real-world cases that increases the accuracy and the size of medical data.

Factor affecting IoT Healthcare Application

There are various factors that affect the IoT healthcare application. Some of them are mention below:

Continuous Research: It requires continuous research in every field (smart devices, fast communication channel, etc.) of healthcare to provide a fast and better facility for patients.

Smart Devices: Need to use the smart device in the healthcare system. IoT opens the potential of current technology and leads us toward new and better medical device solutions.

Better Care: Using IoT technology, healthcare professionals get the enormous data of the patient, analysis the data and facilitate better care to the patient.

Medical Information Distribution: IoT technology makes a transparency of information and distributes the accurate and current information to patients. This leads the fewer accidents from miscommunication, better preventive care, and improved patient satisfaction.

Simple Healthcare System Architecture

The application of the Internet of Things (IoT) in healthcare transforms it into more smart, fast and more accurate. There is different IoT architecture in healthcare that brings start health care system.

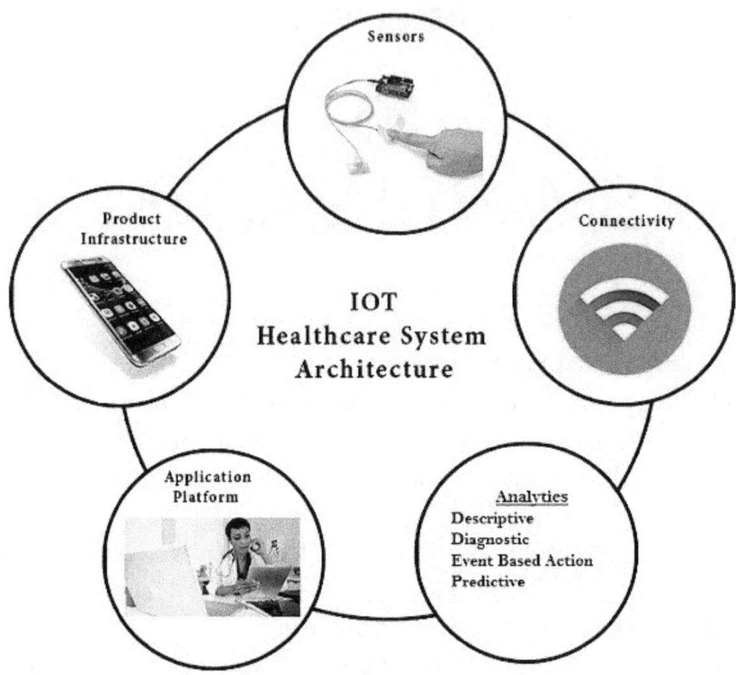

Smart Health

Product Infrastructure: IoT product infrastructure such as hardware/ software component read the sensors signals and display them to a dedicated device.

Sensors: IoT in healthcare has different sensors devices such as pulse-oximeter, electrocardiogram, thermometer, fluid level sensor, sphygmomanometer (blood pressure) that read the current patient situation (data).

Connectivity: IoT system provides better connectivity (using Bluetooth, WiFi, etc.) of devices or sensors from microcontroller to server and vice-versa to read data.

Analytics: Healthcare system analyzes the data from sensors and correlates to get healthy parameters of the patient and on the basis of the analyze data they can upgrade the patient health.

Application Platform: IoT system access information to healthcare professionals on their monitor device for all patients with all details.

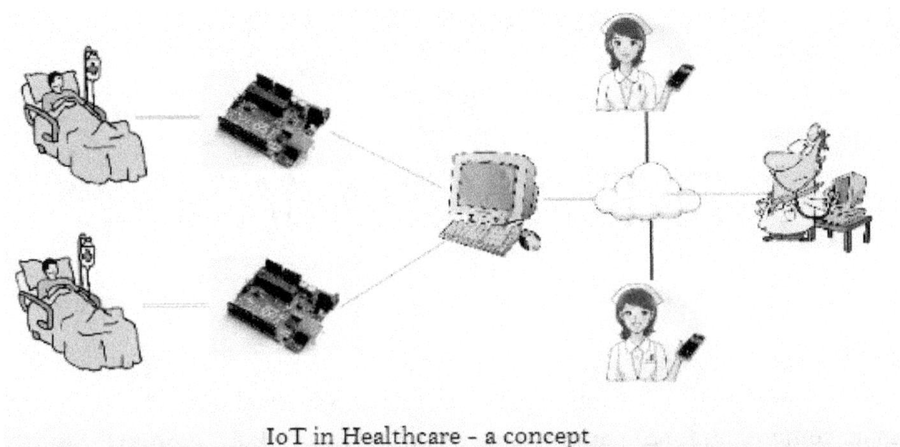

IoT Healthcare

IoT challenges in healthcare

- Data security & privacy
- Integration: multiple devices & protocols
- Data overload & accuracy
- Cost

CHAPTER EIGHT

ENERGY DOMAIN

IoT Energy Domain

The **Internet of Things** plays a vital role in the field of energy management and regulation. The term used for that is **Smart Energy System**. IoT applications monitor a wide variety of energy control function to residential and commercial use.

Residential Energy

As technology is increasing day by day, it also raises the cost of energy. Consumers search the way through which they can reduce and control the energy cost. IoT provides a mature way to analyze and optimize the use of the device as well as the entire system of a home. It may be changing the device setting, simply switching on/off or dimming lights to optimize energy use.

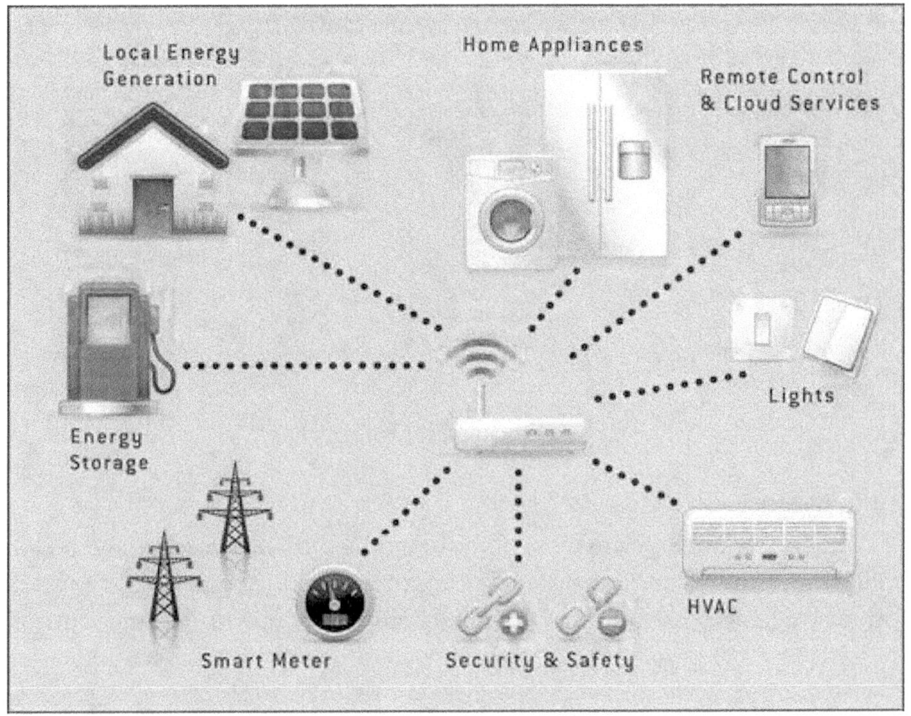

IoT energy domain

Commercial Energy

Wastage of energy widely impacts any business enterprises in their cost of production. IoT provides a specific way for monitoring and maintaining a low cost and high level of care. IoT system provides a strong means of managing the consumption cost of energy and optimize the output of enterprises. It discovers energy issues in the same way as functional issues in a complex business network and provides solutions.

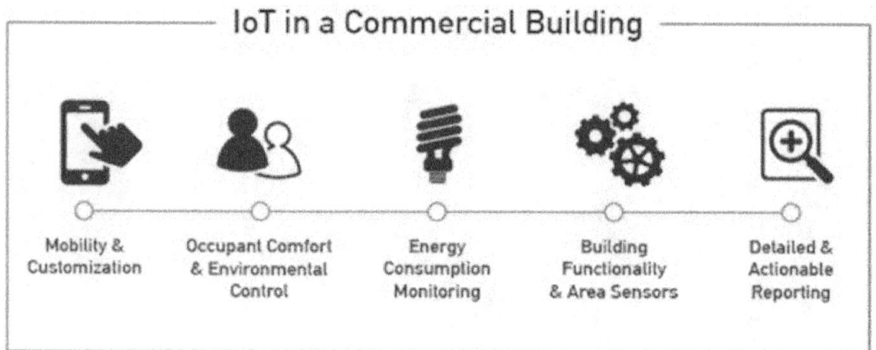

Commercial Energy

Reliability

The IoT technology ensures the system reliability by analytics and action delivered. It detects the threats of system performance and stability which protects against losses such as damaged equipment, downtime, and injuries.

IoT-OTHER FORM OF SMARTNESS

IoT Smart Agriculture Domain

Another important domain for IoT is the agriculture domain where IoT system plays vital role for soil and crop monitoring and provides a proper solution accordingly.

Using smart farming through IoT technologies helps farmer to reduce waste generation and increase the productivity.

There are several IoT technologies available that work on agriculture domain. Some of them are:

Drones for field monitoring

Sensor for soil monitoring

Water pump for water sully

Machines for routine operation

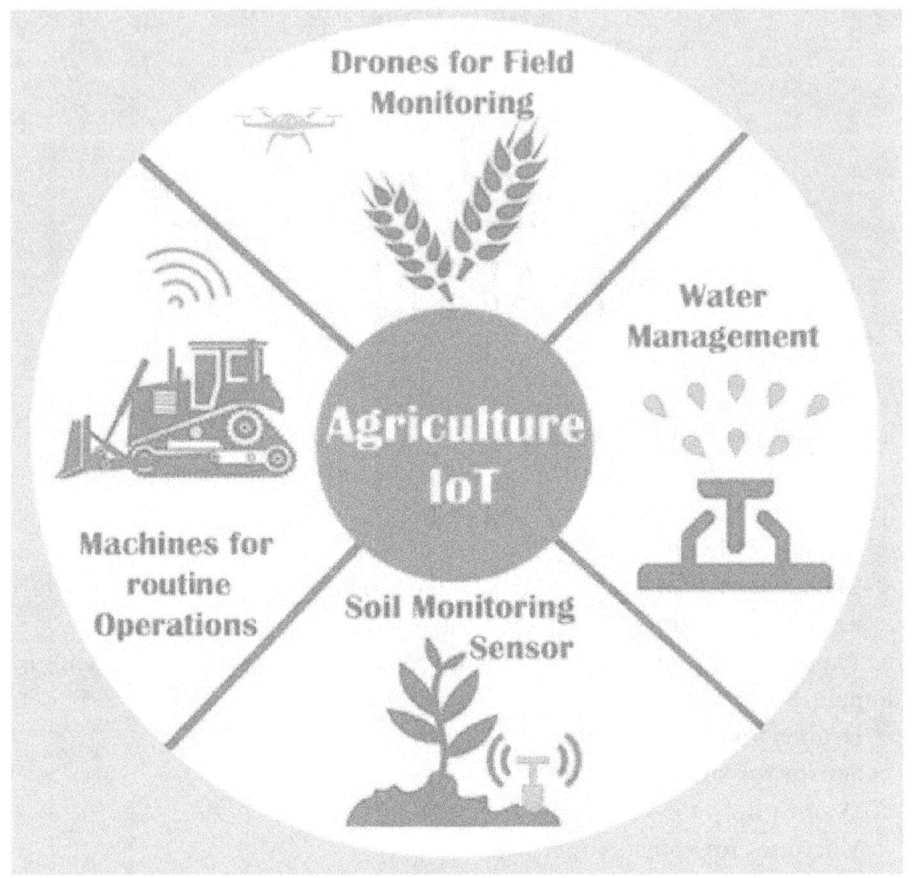

Smart Agriculture

Smart Irrigation System

One of the parts of smart agriculture using IoT is smart irrigation system. In the smart irrigation system, IoT checks the moisture level in the environment or in the water lanes that the farmer has created.

Now, let's understand the working process of this smart irrigation system. Usually, the two main IoT devices that used here is the Arduino board and the Raspberry Pi. The Raspberry Pi becomes the main processing unit, and an Arduino board is placed from each of water channels. These Arduino boards themselves connect to multiple sensors which are part of this water channel so what these sensors check the moisture present in these lanes as such. So, let's say a specific lane does not meet the minimum required moisture then the Arduino board would send a signal to the Raspberry Pi. Again, all these devices are connected on the same wireless router network, and the Raspberry Pi would identify the lack of moisture and pass a signal to the relay. The relay, in turn, would initiate the water pump and the water would be parked now to ensure that water is not wasted. The smart irrigation system would be a gate control system and only that gate will open where the moister is less. Once the sensors detect that the moisture level has gone beyond the required limit, it would again transmit another signal to the Raspberry Pi asking it to stop the pump as well. So, this helps a farmer to save a lot of water and also makes life quite easier as well. So, after this, the farmer only task is to either setting up new plans or creating new water channels.

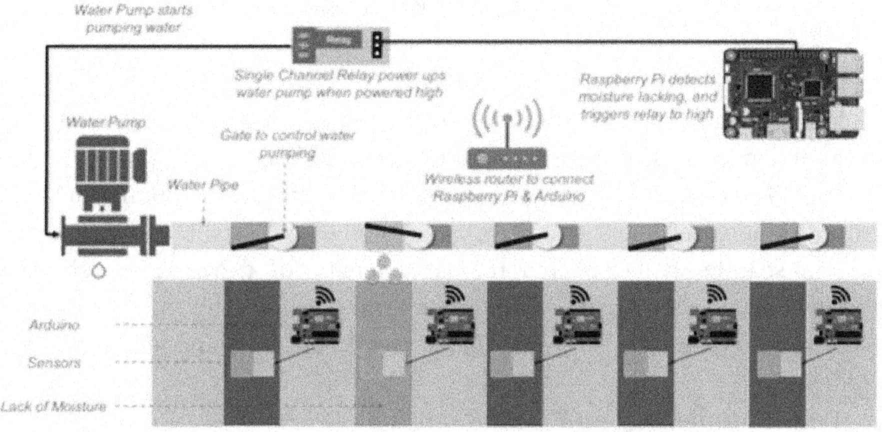

Smart Irrigation

Internet of Things (IoT) in Transportation

Internet of Things (IoT) has crucial applications in the transportation system. IoT plays an important role in all the field of transportation as air-transportation, water-transportation, and land transportation. All the component of these transportation fields is built with smart devices (sensors, processors) and interconnected through cloud server or different servers that transmit data to networks.

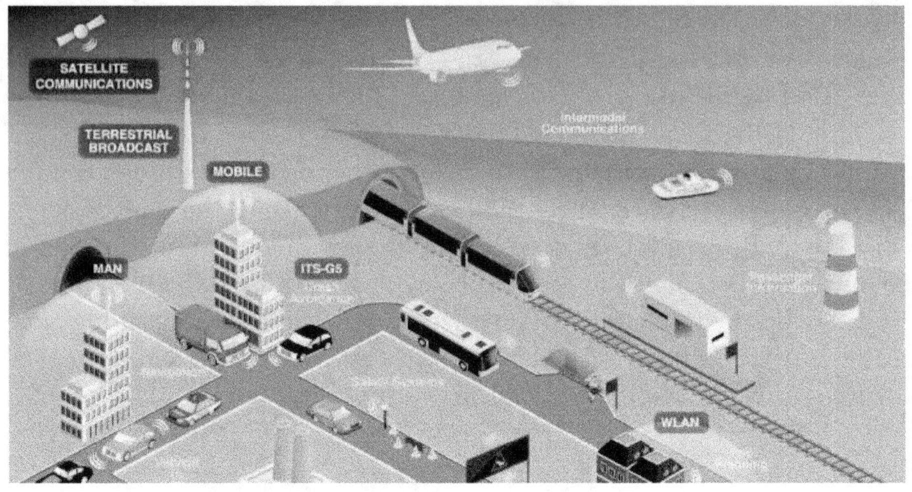

Smart Transportation

Connected to every means of travel

IoT in transportation is not only for traveling from one place to another, but it also makes safer, greener and more convenient. For example, a smart car performs work simultaneously such as navigation, communication, entertainment, efficient, more reliable travel. IoT facilitates travelers to remain seamlessly connected to every means of travel. The vehicle is connected with the variety of wireless standards to the internet such as Bluetooth, Wi-Fi, 3G, 4G, intelligent traffic system, and even to other vehicles.

Traffic Monitoring and Avoid Collision

Sensors built inside or outside a vehicle suggest lane departure and continuously monitor object at all side to avoid the collision. IoT component of transportation does not only mean within the vehicle, but it extends beyond car to communicate other, enabling automate real-time decision to optimize travel. For example, traffic monitoring camera identifies the accident or traffic conjunction and send an alert message to the nearest traffic control room and send current traffic conjunction information to other near vehicles to divert their route.

Smart Traffic

IoT also helps in tracking vehicle current location and distance travel.

CHAPTER TEN

IoT FOR SMART CITIES

The UN predicts that by 2050, the world's urban population is likely to double and reach the point of nearly 6.7 million people. As the number of urban residents grows, cities face new opportunities... And challenges. To prevent environmental deterioration, avoid sanitation problems, mitigate traffic congestion, and thwart urban crime, municipalities turn to the Internet of Things (IoT).

IoT has the potential to tame the pressure of urbanization, create new experience for city residents, and make day-to-day living more comfortable and secure.

In this article, we will share our IoT consulting experience and shed light on the smart city applications, present an optimal approach to the implementation of smart city solutions, as well as explore the peculiarities of rolling out IoT solutions in cities of different sizes.

Smart City

IoT use cases for smart cities

IoT-enabled smart city use cases span multiple areas: from contributing to a healthier environment and improving traffic to enhancing public safety and optimizing street lighting. Below, we provide an overview of the most popular use cases that are already implemented in smart cities across the globe.

Road traffic

Smart cities ensure that their citizens get from point A to point B as safely and efficiently as possible. To achieve this, municipalities turn to IoT development and implement smart traffic solutions.

Smart traffic solutions use different types of sensors, as well as fetch GPS data from drivers' smart phones to determine the number, location and the speed of vehicles. At the same time, smart traffic lights connected to a cloud management platform allow monitoring green light timings and automatically alter the lights based on current traffic situation to prevent congestion. Additionally, using historical data, smart solutions for traffic management can predict where the traffic could go and take measures to prevent potential congestion.

For example, being one of the most traffic-affected cities in the world, Los Angeles has implemented a smart traffic solution to control traffic flow.

Road-surface sensors and closed-circuit television cameras send real-time updates about the traffic flow to a central traffic management platform. The platform analyzes the data and notifies the platform users of congestion and traffic signal malfunctions via desktop user apps. Additionally, the city is deploying a network of smart controllers to automatically make second-by-second traffic lights adjustments, reacting to changing traffic conditions in real time.

Smart parking

With the help of GPS data from drivers' smartphones (or road-surface sensors embedded in the ground on parking spots), smart parking solutions determine whether the parking spots are occupied or available and create a real-time parking map. When the closest parking spot becomes free, drivers receive a notification and use the map on their phone to find a parking spot faster and easier instead of blindly driving around.

Public transport

The data from IoT sensors can help to reveal patterns of how citizens use transport. Public transportation operators can use this data to enhance traveling experience, achieve a higher level of safety and punctuality. To carry out a more sophisticated analysis, smart public transport solutions can combine multiple sources, such as ticket sales and traffic information.

In London, for instance, some train operators predict the loading of train passenger cars on their trips in and out of the city. They combine the data from ticket sales, movement sensors, and CCTV cameras installed along the platform. Analyzing this data, train operators can predict how each car will load up with passengers. When a train comes into a station, train operators encourage passengers to spread along the train to maximize the loading. By maximizing the capacity use, train operators avoid train delays.

Utilities

IoT-equipped smart cities allow citizens to save money by giving them more control over their home utilities. IoT enables different approaches to smart utilities:

Smart meters & billing

With a network of smart meters, municipalities can provide citizens with cost-effective connectivity to utilities companies' IT systems. Now, smart connected meters can send data directly to a public utility over a telecom network, providing it with reliable meter readings. Smart metering allows utilities companies to bill accurately for the amount of water, energy and gas consumed by each household.

Revealing consumption patterns

A network of smart meters enables utilities companies to gain greater visibility and see how their customers consume energy and water. With a network of smart meters, utilities companies can monitor demand in real time and redirect resources as necessary or encourage consumers to use less energy or water at times of shortage.

Remote monitoring

IoT smart city solutions can also provide citizens with utility management services. These services allow citizens to use their smart meters to track and control their usage remotely. For instance, a householder can turn off their home central heating using a mobile phone. Additionally, if a problem (e.g., a water leakage) occurs, utilities companies can notify householders and send specialists to fix it.

Street lighting

IoT-based smart cities make maintenance and control of street lamps more straightforward and cost-effective. Equipping streetlights with sensors and connecting them to a cloud management solution helps to adapt lighting schedule to the lighting zone.

Smart lighting solutions gather data on illuminance, movement of people and vehicles, and combine it with historical and contextual data (e.g., special events, public transport schedule, time of day and year, etc.) and analyze it to improve the lighting schedule. As a result, a smart lighting solution "tells" a streetlight to dim, brighten, switch on or switch off the lights based on the outer conditions.

For instance, when pedestrians cross the road, the lights around the crossings can switch to a brighter setting; when a bus is expected to arrive at a bus stop, the streetlights around it can be automatically set brighter than those further away, etc.

Waste management

Most waste collection operators' empty containers according to predefined schedules. This is not a very efficient approach since it leads to the unproductive use of waste containers and unnecessary fuel consumption by waste collecting trucks.

IoT-enabled smart city solutions help to optimize waste collecting schedules by tracking waste levels, as well as providing route optimization and operational analytics.

Each waste container gets a sensor that gathers the data about the level of the waste in a container. Once it is close to a certain threshold, the waste management solution receives a sensor record, processes it, and sends a notification to a truck driver's mobile app. Thus, the truck driver empties a full container, avoiding emptying half-full ones.

Environment

IoT-driven smart city solutions allow tracking parameters critical for a healthy environment in order to maintain them at an optimal level. For example, to monitor water quality, a city can deploy a network of sensors across the water grid and connect them to a cloud management platform. Sensors measure pH level, the amount of dissolved oxygen and dissolved ions. If leakage occurs and the chemical composition of water changes, the cloud platform triggers an output defined by the users. For example, if a Nitrate (NO_3^-) level exceeds 1 mg/L, a water quality management solution alerts maintenance teams of contamination and automatically creates a case for field workers, who then start fixing the issue.

Another use case is monitoring air quality. For that, a network of sensors is deployed along busy roads and around plants. Sensors gather data on the amount of CO, nitrogen, and sulfur oxides, while the central cloud platform analyzes and visualizes sensor readings, so that platform users can view the map of air quality and use this data to point out areas where air pollution is critical and work out recommendations for citizens.

Public safety

For enhancing public safety, IoT-based smart city technologies offer real-time monitoring, analytics, and decision-making tools. Combining data from acoustic sensors and CCTV cameras deployed throughout the city with the data from social media feed and analyzing it, public safety solutions can predict potential crime scenes. This will allow the police to stop potential perpetrators or successfully track them.

For example, more than 90 cities across the United States use a gunshot detection solution. The solution uses connected microphones installed throughout a city. The data from microphones passes over to the cloud platform, which analyzes the sounds and detects a gunshot. The platform measures the time it took for the sound to reach the microphone and estimates the location of the gun. When the gunshot and its location are identified, cloud software alerts the police via a mobile app.

Iterative approach to implementing smart city solutions

The range of smart city applications is highly diverse. What they have in common is the approach to implementation. Whether municipalities plan to automate waste collection or improve street lighting, they should start with the foundation – a basic smart city platform. If a municipality prefers to expand the range of smart city services in future, it will be possible to upgrade the existing architecture with new tools and technologies without having to rebuild it.

Here is a six-step implementation model to follow for creating an efficient and scalable IoT architecture for a smart city.

Stage 1: basic IoT-based smart city platform

To be able to scale, smart city implementation should start with designing a basic architecture – it will serve as a springboard for future enhancements and allow adding new services without losing functional performance. A basic IoT solution for smart cities includes four components:

The network of smart things

A smart city – as any IoT system – uses smart things equipped with sensors and actuators. The immediate goal of *sensors* is to collect data and pass it to a central cloud management platform. *Actuators* allow devices to act - alter the lights, restrict the flow of water to the pipe with leakage, etc.

Gateways

Any IoT system comprises two parts – a "tangible" part of IoT devices and network nodes and a cloud part. The data cannot simply pass from one part to the other. There must be doors – *field gateways*. Field gateways facilitate data gathering and compression by preprocessing and filtering data before moving it to the cloud. *The cloud gateway* ensures secure data transmission between field gateways and the cloud part of a smart city solution.

Data lake

The main purpose of a data lake is to store data. Data lakes preserve data in its raw state. When the data is needed for meaningful insights, it's extracted and passed over to the big data warehouse.

Big data warehouse

A big data warehouse is a single data repository. Unlike data lakes, it contains only structured data. Once the value of data has been defined, it's extracted, transformed and loaded into the big data warehouse. Moreover, it stores contextual information about connected things, e.g., when sensors were installed, as well as the commands sent to devices' actuators by control applications.

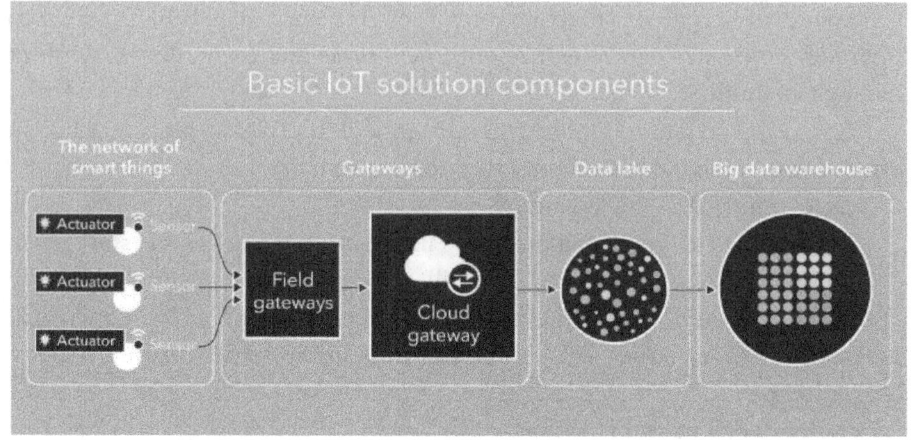

Smart City Platform

Stage 2: Monitoring and basic analytics

With data analytics, it is possible to monitor devices' environment and set rules for control applications (we cover them at stage 4) to carry out a particular task.

For example, analyzing the data from soil moisture sensors deployed across <u>a smart park</u>, cities can set rules for the electronic valves to close or open based on the identified moisture level. The data collected with sensors can be visualized on a single platform dashboard, allowing users to know the current state of each park zone.

Stage 3: Deep analytics

Processing IoT-generated data, city administrations can go beyond monitoring & basic analytics and identify *patterns* and hidden *correlations* in sensor data. Data analytics uses advanced techniques like machine learning (ML) and statistical analysis. ML algorithms analyze historical sensor data stored in the big data warehouse to identify trends and create predictive models based on them. The models are used by control applications that send commands to IoT devices' actuators. Here is how it applies in practice.

Unlike a traditional traffic light that is programmed to display a particular signal for a definite period, a smart traffic light can adapt signal timings to the traffic scenario. ML algorithms are applied to historical sensor data to reveal traffic patterns and adjust signal timings, helping to improve average vehicle speed and avoid congestions.

Stage 4: Smart control

Control applications ensure better automation of smart city objects by sending *commands* to their *actuators*. Basically, they "tell" actuators what to do to solve a particular task. There are *rule-based* and *ML-based* control applications. Rules for rule-based control applications are defined manually, while ML-based control applications use models created by ML algorithms. These models are identified based on data analysis; they are tested, approved and regularly updated.

Stage 5: Instant interacting with citizens via user applications

Along with the possibility of automated control, there should always be an option for users to influence the behavior of smart city applications (for example, in case of emergency). This task is carried out by user applications.

User applications allow citizens to connect to the central smart city management platform to monitor and control IoT devices, as well as receive notifications and alerts. For example, using GPS data from drivers' smartphones, a smart traffic management solution identifies a traffic jam. To prevent even bigger congestion, the solution automatically sends a notification to the drivers in the area, encouraging them to take a different route.

At the same time, employees at a traffic control center who use a desktop user app receive a 'congestion alert.' To relieve the congestion and re-route part of the traffic, they send a command to the traffic lights' actuators to alter the signals.

Stage 6: Integrating several solutions

Achieving "smartness" is not a one-time action – it is a continuous process. Implementing IoT-based smart city solutions today, municipalities should think of services they might like to implement tomorrow. It implies not only increasing the number of sensors but, more importantly, the number of functions. Let's illustrate this functional scalability with the example of a smart city solution for traffic monitoring.

A city deploys a traffic management solution to detect traffic jams in real time and manage traffic lights to reduce traffic in the areas with intensive traffic. After some time, the city decides to ensure city traffic doesn't harm the environment and integrates the traffic management solution with a smart air quality monitoring solution. Cross-solution integration allows controlling both traffic and air quality in the city dynamically.

For that, traffic lights or street lights along the roads can be equipped with sensors that monitor air quality. Sensors measure the amount of CO, NO, and NO2 in the air and pass data records to a central air quality management platform for processing. If the amount of harmful gases in the air is critical, control applications apply rules or use models to take an output action, e.g., 'alter traffic lights.' Before that, there is a need to make sure that altering traffic lights won't cause accidents or blockages in other areas. It is possible due to the integration of the traffic management solution to the air quality management solution. The traffic management platform performs real-time analysis and identifies if it is possible to alter the traffic lights. If altering the lights is acceptable, control applications send a command to the traffic lights' actuators, which execute the command.

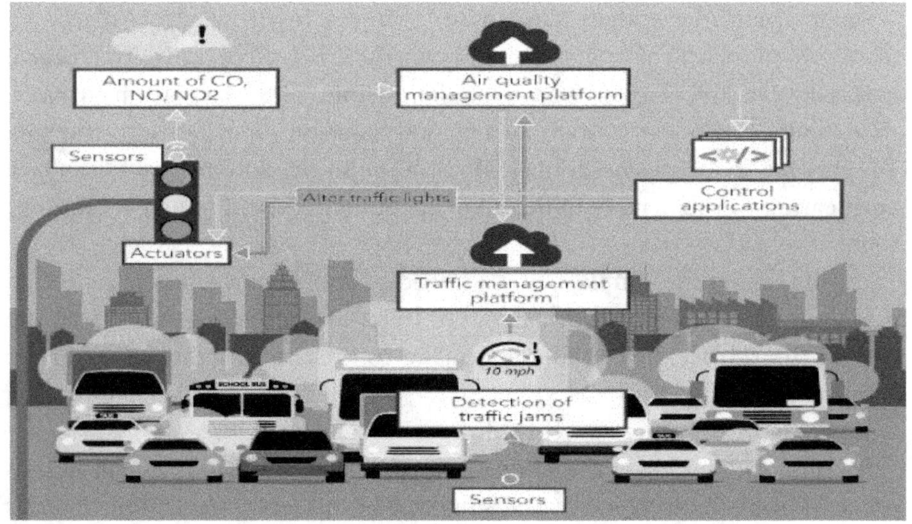

Smart City Solution

Applying an iterative approach helps municipalities to reduce implementation costs, get a faster pay-off and make the benefits of smart solutions visible for citizens sooner.

Adapting IoT implementation strategy to the city size

Iterative approach can be leveraged in cities of different sizes. In larger ones, it helps to deal with the scale and complexity of implementation; in smaller ones, it helps to reduce investments in smart solutions and use constrained infrastructure resources more reasonably. However, starting a smart project in a smaller city, municipalities have some more points to consider.

On the way to smartness, midsized and small cities face many barriers, including budgetary and procurement shortages, limited resources for public services, under-resourced IT infrastructure, etc. However, it doesn't mean a smaller city cannot be a smart city.

Starting a smart initiative in a city of medium or small size, it makes sense to begin with the projects that do not require huge investments and deliver tangible return on investments, such as smart parking or waste management, and use the established infrastructure to implement new services.

For example, the town of Vail, CO has less than 6,000 inhabitants but boasts an extensive smart infrastructure. The town started smart city development with connected streetlights. Later, they used the established infrastructure to broaden the range of services and topped it with smart parking and irrigation systems.

To determine which applications are a good fit for smaller cities, we've analyzed them by the volume of investments, required infrastructure, pay-off period, the visibility of benefits for citizens and came up with the following table:

THE RELEVANCE OF IOT APPLICATIONS FOR SMALLER SMART CITIES			
	Highly relevant	Can be implemented with certain restrictions	The value is questionable
Traffic management			●
Parking	●		
Public transport		●	
Utilities			●
Street lightning	●		
Waste management	●		
Environment		●	
Public safety		●	

Different sized smart cities

Another non-trivial way to enhance the affordability and accessibility of smart applications is sharing a common platform with a larger city. The cloud nature of IoT-enabled smart city solutions is suitable for that. This way, smart city solutions of both large and smaller smart cities are connected to and managed via a single cloud platform. By sharing the platform based on open data, several smart cities form a common urban ecosystem. One of the examples of such sharing is the Iberian Smart Cities Network, which currently includes 111 cities in Portugal and Spain.

The network comprises cities of different sizes, which cooperate in multiple areas including smart energy, mobility, environment, and transport.

Let's Sum It Up

IoT helps cities connect and manage multiple infrastructure and public services. From smart lighting and road traffic to connected public transport and waste management – the range of use cases is highly diverse. What they have in common is the outcomes. Applying IoT solutions leads to reduced costs for energy, optimized use of natural resources, safer cities, and a healthier environment.

However, to enjoy these benefits, municipalities should take a consistent approach to design a functional and scalable smart city architecture. Well-designed, it will allow to reduce investments in IoT development and hasten the implementation of smart city solutions, still leaving space for expansion.